Pioneer
Free Will Baptists
Ministers
Burial Locations
In
Maine

Copyright 2016
By
Dr. Alton E. Loveless

ISBN 978-1523619047 Soft cover

2020 Update

This book was printed in the United States of America.

To order additional copies of this book, contact:
FWB Publications
Enchanting Acres
1006 Rayme Drive
Columbus, Ohio 43207
Alton.loveless@prodigy.net
Or
www.amazon.com

FWB
FWB Publications

Introduction

Maine

This book represents all that were part of the Free Will Baptist movement, consisting of the Palmer (south), Randall (north) and others such as the Stone, John-Thomas, John Wheeler Assns., NC OFWB and more.

Many of the photos are poor quality, but it was all I could find. Likewise, I do not have photos or tombstones for many of them. The information about these ministers were all that was available to me or found in archives. I made every effort to include those for which they would be remembered. Some I had no information, but research had shown they were of our denomination.

This Section is taken for a two Volume set done by this author.

Maine

George J Abbot
Born
Dec. 3, 1830
Death:
Nov. 3, 1883
Burial:
Pond Cemetery 1, Unity,
Waldo County, Maine,
Plot: row 6

He was baptized by the Rev. Dexter Waterman, under whose labors he was converted about 1852. He joined the church in South Jackson, Maine and in June of 1856 he was licensed by the Unity quarterly meeting. Soon after this, he went to the theological school at new Hampton, New Hampshire where he was highly esteemed by his teachers and fellow students. He was ordained in June of 1858 during a session of that same quarterly meeting. His pastorates were in South Montville, Wayne, and Dover, Maine and also in Bristol, Hampton, New Hampshire. He was pastor of the Apponaug church in this state of Rhode Island. The Rev. E Knowlton, a well-known Free Will Baptists at the time, knew him in his first church and said of him that he was one of the best spirited man he had ever known and for a young man his sermons were both spiritual and instructive.

John Quincy Adams
Birth:
Jan. 19, 1848
Death:
Apr. 16, 1897
Burial:
Riverside Cemetery, Lewiston,
Androscoggin County, Maine

He graduated from Bates College 1876 and from the Divinity school in 1881. He was baptized by the Rev. Elisha Purington, his pastor. In April, before his graduation, he accepted the call to the South Parsonsfield, Maine church. He also pastored a church in Dover, Maine, but due to failing health he resided in Lewiston and supplied the Kennebunk and Kennebunk Port churches for one year. In 1883 he was a delegate to the General Conference from the Maine Western quarterly meeting. In 1885 and 1886 he was the corresponding secretary of the Maine Association and delivered addresses at its annual meetings.

William Abbott

Birth:
1793
Livermore
Androscoggin County, Maine
Death:
Jul. 16, 1877
New Portland
Somerset County, Maine
Burial:
East New Portland Cemetery
New Portland, Somerset County,
Maine

He became a Christian when about 26, was baptized by Rev. Samuel Hutchins and united with the church in New Portland. He was a faithful minister for over fifty years and instrumental in bringing many to Christ. He was a strong advocate of education and reforms. He won the affection of his brethren by whom he was venerated.

Moses Ames

Birth:
Dec. 8, 1812
Dover-Foxcroft,
Piscataquis, Maine
Death:
Sep. 30, 1860
South Dover, Me.
Burial:
South Dover Cemetery
Dover-Foxcroft
Piscataquis County, Maine
Plot: North Section, Row 2

Moses Ames was a FWB clergyman, At the age of 4, the family moved to Bradford, where after twelve years his parents were reclaimed, and he had the conviction strongly forced upon his heart that he was a sinner. In the spring of 1834, through a protracted meeting, he and others were converted, and in July following he began preaching. He had been baptized by Rev. Nathaniel Harvey, uniting with the church in Bradford. The destitute churches in the Sebec Q. Y. were objects of his labor. He was licensed by the Quarterly Meeting September, 1838, and labored in Garland and Danville. Sept. 22, 1839, he was ordained. In May 1838, he began his ministry at Corinth. In 1840 he saw from his preaching a great revival at Garland, and in a short time baptized over twenty. His work in Bradford was blessed. In 1841 he saw revivals both in the Wellington and in the Springfield Q. M's. In October he was present at the eleventh General Conference at Topsham. He moved his family to

Corinth in December, where for some months he had preached half the time. In January 1842, in a revival at Hunting's Mills, in Corinth, twenty-three were added to the church. A revival attended him in Garland where he preached part of the time. During the summer he baptized there forty-six. and in 1845 moved there. He attended the thirteenth General Conference in Sutton, Vt., in October 1847, as a delegate from the Penobscot Y. M. The next year he moved to Veazie for a pastorate of two years. Here a church was organized. In November 1850, he began his labors with the Dover and Foxcroft church, where his strength failed him. During the last year of his ministry seventy were added to the church. He was a man highly gifted in natural talent; he possessed good business ability. His devotion to the ministry cost him his health. He was a gifted speaker and drew multitudes after him.

"His Power Is Infinitely Strong,

So Is His Wisdom Infinitely Clear,

And His Will Infinitely Pure."

Otis Andrews
Birth:
Mar. 14, 1817
Livermore Falls
Androscoggin County, Maine
Death:
May 5, 1897
Industry
Franklin County,Maine
Burial:
Weeks Mills Cemetery
New Sharon
Franklin County, Maine

He studied in the common schools and was converted on January 1, 1836. He was licensed in 1838 and then ordained by the Bowdoin Quarterly Meeting In 1843. He pastored a number of churches and enjoyed many revival meetings. He saw 100's converted, married over 100 couples and attended over 200 funerals.
Inscription:
REV. OTIS ANDREWS
MAR. 14, 1817-MAY 5, 1897

Hezekiah Atwood
Birth:
unknown
Death:
Dec. 26, 1870
Burial:
Gibbs Mill Cemetery
Livermore
Androscoggin County, Maine

He studied at the Farmington Academy and served his denomination for many years in the state of Maine. He organized the church at Barkers Island, Booth Bay, Maine. He had a son A. C. Atwood that was a pastor in Cape Sable Island, Nova Scotia.

Inscription:
HEZEKIAH ATWOOD
Died
Dec. 26, 1870
AGE. 72

Aaron Ayer
Birth:
Apr. 3, 1802
Buxton, York County, Maine
Death:
Oct. 8, 1866
Naples
Cumberland County, Maine
Burial:
Naples Village Cemetery
Naples, Cumberland County, Maine

Ayer was a Freewill Baptist Minister. He filled pulpits in Maine and New Hampshire, and was widely known and beloved. (His stone says 1866).

Inscription:
AARON AYER
Died Oct. 8, 1866
Age. 64 yrs. 5 mos.
Blessed are the dead that die in the Lord.

Rev James M. Bailey
Birth:
Mar. 3, 1817
Andover, Merrimack County
New Hampshire
Death:
1899
Burial:
Hillcrest Cemetery
West Buxton
York County, Maine

Rev. J.M. Bailey, D.D., was ordained a gospel minister in the Freewill Baptist church in Feb. 1847. He was an active and useful minister.

John M Bailey
Birth:
1764
Death:
Oct. 5, 1857
Burial:
Grover Cemetery
Woolwich, Sagadahoc County,
Maine

He was born in Woolwich in 1764, and was converted by the preaching of Benjaman Randall and baptized by Rev. E. Lock about 1787. In 1798, when the denomination had less than a score of ministers, he was ordained by Timothy Cnnningham and Dea. Daniel Dunton, neither of whom were then ordained ministers. He entered upon a long ministry. In 1823, the best of feeling was restored by the aid of a council between him and his church, and with the help of Rev. Allen Files a revival sprung up in which over 100 were converted. He retained his mental faculties to the end of his long and useful life, and died in peace, fully resigned to his Master's will. Revolutionary War veteran.An ordained Freewill Baptist minister, died at age 93 years.

Rev Nathaniel Bard
Birth:
Sep. 2, 1814
Sumner
Oxford County
Maine
Death:
May 30, 1874

Lisbon
Androscoggin County
Maine
Burial:
Hillside Cemetery
Lisbon Falls
Androscoggin County, Maine

Rev. Nathaniel Bard, was a resident of Lisbon about forty years. When about 20 years of age he became a Christian, was baptized by Rev. Charles Bean, and united with the Second church of Lisbon. He was licensed by the Bowdoin Quarterly Meeting (QM) in 1840, and at the end of that year, was ordained.

He preached in Webster, Wales, Oak Hill, Litchfield two years, Litchfield Plains two yrs. Durham 8 yrs., Richmond Corner several yrs. North Freeport three different times, eight yrs in all; and lastly at Monmout, where an attack of paralysis disabled him and finally terminated his life. Ordained Freewill Baptist minister of Maine. Death listed in the minutes of the 22nd Gen. Conference.

Quite a number were added to the Litchfield churches: many were converted at Durham, and a house of worship was built. At Freeport he had frequent conversions and forty were baptized in one year. Two small churches in Bowdoinham were united by him; the Lisbon Falls church was organized mostly by his labors.

What he may have lacked in early educational mental culture was largely made up for by prayerful study of the Bible, and general reading. He was a man of superior judgment, and a sound gospel preacher. He occupied a prominent place in his Quarterly Meeting, and achieved that distinction by faithful and persistent labor. He was also esteemed for his integrity, kindness and hospitality.

John J. Banks
Birth:
Dec. 20, 1826
Levant, Penobscot County, Maine
Death:
Mar. 13, 1917
Burial:
Corinthian Cemetery,
Penobscot
County,

Maine,
Plot: Div. 9 Lot 8

He became a Christian at the age of 26. He was two years a member of a Baptist church. He received license on Sept. 29, 1855, and on Jan. 3, 1857, was ordained by the Free Will Baptist Springfield Quarterly Meeting. He had a revival in Lincoln, Me, in 1856, and raised up a church of thirty-six members of which he was chosen pastor. In 1858, he had a revival in Chester. He had a revival in Kenduskeag in 1866. A church was organized there two years later of which he has been pastor. He supplied the Congregationalist church of Kenduskeag part time eight years.

John Batchelder
Birth:
Feb. 15, 1813
Rhode Island
Death:
Jun. 21, 1865
Burial:
Evergreen Cemetery,
Garland,
Penobscot County, Maine

John Batchelder moved to New Hampshire at the death of his father in 1823, and went out as a tanner's apprentice. At the age of 21 he was baptized, joining the Free Baptist Church. Having moved to Garland, Maine, he united with the church there in April 1842. He was licensed by the Exeter Q.M.in March 1854 and for a while was connected with the Biblical School at New Hampton. He was ordained in Parkman, Maine in January 1858, in which field he organized a church and became it's pastor. During the last four years of his life his work was crippled through ill health. His last season was spent with the church at South Dover. He was a good preacher and was much beloved.

Inscription:
Died at age 53 yrs. and 4 mos.

Favel Bartlett
Birth:
Apr. 12, 1792
Plymouth, Mass.
Death:
Mar. 22, 1873
Auburn, Me
Burial:
Norway Pine Grove Cemetery
Paris,
Oxford County, Maine

In early manhood he was an active minister in Franklin County, Me., but disease of the throat and lungs forced him to turn aside and engage in business. He became a merchant, but preached occasionally as long as health permitted. Fifteen years before his death he moved to Auburn, where he soon retired from business, in still feebler health. He lived a quiet, cheerful, Christian life till his departure, and was much respected and beloved.

Rev Isaac N Bates
Birth:
Dec. 25, 1830
Waterville
Kennebec County
Maine
Death:
Mar. 28, 1902
Maine
Burial:
Old Cemetery
Oakland
Kennebec County
Mainne

Rev. Isaac N. BATES, was he son of Isaac and Betsy Bates.

He studied in schools at Norridgewock and Waterville, Maine. Converted in March, 1846, he was licensed in 1862, and ordained in 1864. He has had] nine revivals, organized six churches and baptized over 300. He is now settled with the church at Fairfield, Maine.

Rev Charles Bean
Birth:
Jan. 3, 1811
Limerick, Maine
Death: Jun. 18, 1889
Burial:
Highland Cemetery
Buxton
York County, Maine
Plot: Ordained as evangelist
Nov 21, 1833

He received licensed to preach in 1831, and at age 20, was ordained by a council of the Parsonfield Quarterly Meeting.

After itinerat ministry for some years, he became pastor of the Falmouth church and remained three years. He was pastor of several other churches, following this, and after sixty years of ministerial work made his name familiar in western Maine. He preached up to the advanced age of 78, and was noted for a remarkable 'verbatim know-ledge of the Bible.

He died at the residence of his daughter, Mrs. Simon Libby, in Scarborough, ME, June 18, 1889, in his 79th year.

Rev George Winthrop Bean

Birth:
Feb. 8, 1819
Readfield
Kennebec County
Maine, USA
Death:
May 4, 1893
Burial:
Readfield Corner Cemetery
Readfield
Kennebec County,Maine

Ordained in June 1843 as a Free Will Baptist minister at Milton, ME.
Inscription:
His Stone Reads:
God's Church They Lead
Her Stone Reads:
With God They Dwell

Rev Selden Bean

Birth:
1825
Death:
Jul. 6, 1883
Burial:
Seavey's Corner Cemetery
Vienna
Kennebec County
Maine

Age 58 yrs at death. An ordained Freewill Bapt.

Rev Leroy S, Bean

Birth:
Jan. 12, 1860
Quebec, Canada
Death:
Jul. 12, 1903
Maine
Burial:
Laurel Hill Cemetery
Saco
York County
Maine

He was only 43yrs, and a promising young minister. Pastored in Canada, VT and ME.

Charles E. Blake

Birth:
Unknown
Death:
Jan. 8, 1892
Burial:
Riverside Cemetery
Farmington
Franklin County,
Maine

He was a Free Baptist Minister and the father of Rev. Edwin Blake of the same denomination.

Edwin Blake

Birth:
1843
Death:
1915
Burial:
Riverside Cemetery, Farmington,
Franklin County, Maine
Freewill Baptist minister. He served Co. A 8th Me. Vol. Sept. 1861 to Nov. 1865 during the Civil War. His wife was Elsie W. Cross, who lived between 1842-1926.

Stephen S Bowden

Birth:
Oct. 18, 1806
Penobscot, Maine
Death:
Nov. 3, 1878
West Waterville, Maine
Burial:
Old Cemetery
Oakland
Kennebec County, Maine

He was converted in 1829, when 22 years of age, under the labor of Rev. Cyrus Stilson and baptized by him on November 22 and joined the church. He was chosen clerk of the church and served it for 12 years. He was licensed on January 15, 1842. His ordination occurred at the Pittsfield church in June 1844. While not specifically an evangelist, he did have a circuit of some 12 towns in the Waterville Quarterly Meeting and was graciously favored by his ministry. For 30 years before his death he rarely spent a Sunday at home, though few loved home more ardently or more fully honored the relationship of husband and father. His preaching was sound, clear, and persuasive. He attended many funerals and solemnized many marriages. At the time of his death he was clerk of the Quarterly Meeting and had served in this office 17 1/2 years out of the last 20 attending every session. He was chosen delegate to the last General Conference before his death but yielded his place to his alternate.

Rev David Boyd

Birth:
1781
South Berwick, Maine
Death:
Dec. 11, 1855
North Berwick, ME
Burial:
Boyd Plot, South Berwick
York County, Maine

He was one of the Fathers in habits, views of duty, doctrine, styles of communication, and sympathies. He was frequently called to positions of public trust; was a member of the Massachusetts Legislature from Maine, and a member of the convention which framed Maines's Constitution. See "Constitution of Maine" of which Rev. David Boyd was a member in 1820 when it was adopted.

He was familiar with probate matters and other technicalities of law. He was an esteemed Christian.

Rev David Boyd
Birth:
Mar. 2, 1836
Maine, USA
Death:
Mar. 7, 1900
Burial:
Riverside Cemetery
Newport
Penobscot County
Maine

Ordained a Freewill Bapt. minister May 12, 1861.

Aldolphus Eugene Boynton
Birth:
Aug. 5, 1833
Plymouth
Grafton County
New Hampshire
Death:
Sep. 24, 1889
Shapleigh
York County
Maine
Burial:
Pleasant Hill Cemetery
Newfield
York County
Maine

Adolphus Eugene Boynton, Free Baptist, son of John and Phebe (Batchelder) Boynton, was born Aug. 5, 1833. Preparatory studies at New Hampton Institution. Studied for the ministry at Bates (Me.) Theological School. Licensed to preach, Canaan, 1870. Ordained, Newport, Canada, June 21, 1874, and pastor there, and at Eaton, Jan. 1874-5; Daniel's Mills, Newfield, Me., Aug. 1875-8; Kittery Point, Me., June 1878-80; Bow Lake, Strafford, April 1880-1 ; Nottingham, April 1881-2; Barrington and West Notting ham, May 1882-3; North Shapleigh, Me., March 1884-6. Died there, Sept. 24, 1889.From Native Ministry of New Hampshire by Nathan Franklin Carter page 74. Available from FWB Publications.

The resurrection of the body is the final step in our salvation.

Rev James Boyd
Birth:
Nov. 26, 1830
South Berwick, ME
Death:
Oct. 14, 1907
Burial:
Boyd Plot
South Berwick
York County
Maine

His parents were Charles and Margaret (David) BOYD. His education was received in common and select schools. He became a Christian at the age of twenty-one, and was baptized by Rev. C.B. Mills. He received license to preach in December, 1855, and was ordained in December, 1856, by Rev. E. Knowlton, and others at the Unity Quarterly Meeting (Q.M.). He held pastorates in Bangor (Second Church), Sabattus, Booth Bay, Biddeford, ME; Taunton, Mass; Bangor ME, (First Church), and Pittsfield, ME. He was a state missionary of Maine, New Hampshire, Massachusetts, Rhode Island, New York, and Wisconsin. He was a missionary pastor at several churches including Cape Sable Island, and Halifax. N.S., and Manchester, N.H. He has baptized over 300, with more than that number converted. Helped ordain Rev. V. D. Sweetland in 1879.

He was married Sept. 4, 1851, to Miss Mary M. Cuttings. Of eight children, four are living [1889]. His son, Charles S. Boyd was a member of the class of 1881 in Bates Theological School when he died.

Rev David Brackett
Birth:
Feb. 1, 1837
Jackson
Waldo County
Maine
Death:
1922
Burial:
Grove Cemetery
Belfast
Waldo County
Maine,

Rev. David Brackett, Jr., son of David and Olive (Trueworthy) Brackett, was born in Jackson, ME in 1837. He was converted at the age of forty-three. The next year, 1881, he received license to preach, and in 1882 was ordained at the Quarterly Meeting. He had a revival in the Brooks church in 1881, and in the Thorndike and Knox churches in 18882-83, of which he became pastor of the Thorndike church.

Levi Brackett

Birth:
1813
Westbrook, Maine
Death:
1890
Burial:
Growstown Cemetery
Brunswick
Cumberland County, Maine

He was converted at age 26, and graduated from the Theological School at Whitestown, New York about 10 years afterwards in 1849. He received license to preach in 1844 and was ordained by the Bowdoin quarterly Meeting in 1849. After pastoring in New Hampshire for many years he moved to West Lebanon, Maine and supplied in Northfield and elsewhere. He also pastored in North Parsonsfield. Revivals and baptisms he enjoyed in nearly in all his pastorates. On December 20 field, 1852 he married Mrs. Nancy J Cram, of Brownfield, Maine. He had four children and the oldest was a professor at the Colorado State University. The older daughter was a teacher in the Classical Institute at Hallowell, Maine, and the second daughter is Librarian of the Spear Library at Oberlin College. These three were graduates of Bates College, Lewiston Maine.

Nancy Jane Cram Brackett
Birth:
1827
Death:
1897
Burial:

Growstown Cemetery
Brunswick
Cumberland County, Maine

She had been a Free Will Baptist preacher prior to the marriage to Rev. Levi Brackett.

Me Rev Allen W Bradeen
Birth:
Feb. 27, 1859
Maine, USA
Death:
1915
Springvale
York County
Maine
Burial:
Mount Pleasant Cemetery
Dexter
Penobscot County
Maine

Rev. Allen W. Bradeen, son of Isaac and Philena C. (Billington) Bradeen, was born at Byron ME, Feb. 27,

1859. He studied at the Wilton Academy 1882-84, and at Cobb Divinity School 1884-88. In the winter of 1878 he was converted, and licensed Jan 11, 1887. He has supplied at Hallowell, ME, and during one year five were baptized and seven admitted into the church. In 1888 he became pastor at Dexter, ME, and was ordained.

Rev Frank C. Bradeen
Birth:
Jun. 29, 1840
Maine
Death:
Nov. 4, 1923
Burial:
Highland Cemetery
Buxton
York County, Maine

An ordained Free Will Baptist minister and pastor in Maine and New Hampshire; ordained ca 1873, after which he ministered to the Dexter Village, Exeter and St. Albans churches, and in 1877, went to Parsonfield. He pastored in Concord N.H. the Curtis Mem.

Rev Roscoe E Bradford
Birth:
Sep. 8, 1857
Death:
Jul. 29, 1889
Burial:
Knox Station Cemetery
Knox
Waldo County
Maine

Ordained Free Will Baptist minister/pastor in Maine 1883); studied (1887 to ?) in Bates Theological School, Lewiston ME.

Rev Otis W Bridges
Birth:
Jan. 26, 1806
Penobscot, ME
Death:
Oct. 24, 1903
Burial:
Mount Pleasant Cemetery
Dexter
Penobscot County
Maine

His parents were Rev. Abiezer and Deborah (Stores) Bridges. He was converted at the age of seventeen. He received license to preach in 1830, and was ordained in 1834, by Rev's Clement Phinney (who preached the sermon), Benjamin Thorn, and A. Files, of the Bowdoin Quarterly Meeting. He lived in Sangerville, ME, forty-two years, where he labored in a number of revivals, and assisted in organizing two churches. He resided at Ft. Fairfield, and was pastor of the church there. He was married Oct. 11, 1833 to Margaret W. Owen, and has three children; his oldest son is a deacon of the Dexter church

Ebenezer Brown
Birth:
1771
Death:
Mar. 27, 1838
Wilton, ME,
Burial:
East Wilton Cemetery
Wilton
Franklin County, Maine

Rev. Ebenezer BROWN, d. at age 67 yrs. He was ordained a minister of the Freewill Baptist church May 19, 1805. He was married to Hannah, who d. May 29, 1852, age 76. Their daughter, Hannah (Brown) Fletcher, m. Asa Fletcher Jan. 27, 1877. Brown, after a pastorate of the First church at for many years died after a hurtful and distressing illness. He was excellent as a counselor, and zealous in his work for the Savior.

Rev Albion C Brown
Birth:
Jan. 13, 1859
New Portland
Somerset County
Maine
Death:
1944
Burial:
Oak Grove Cemetery
Bath
Sagadahoc County
Maine
Plot: South 4

Son of Israel and Flora A. (Emery) Brown. They mar. Nov. 1, 1857, at New Portland, Somerset Co. ME.
Rev. A.C. Brown was ordained to the ministry June 29, 1887, and pastored Vienna Church, Weeks Mills, and First Mount Vernon Church.

Jonathan Brown
Birth:
1772
Death:
Sep. 10, 1850
Burial:
Curtis Cemetery, Bowdoinham, Sagadahoc County, Maine

Jonathan Brown was born in Phippsburgh, ME. At the age of twelve he was converted and baptized. About the year 1803 he began to preach. He was ordained to the Free Baptist ministry in 1808. He was afflicted through much sickness in his family, but as far as possible, he prosecuted his holy calling.

Georges E S Bryant
Birth:
October 28, 1818
Dover-Foxcroft,
Piscataquis, Maine
Death:
1871
Burial:
South Dover Cemetery
Dover-Foxcroft
Piscataquis County, Maine
Plot: North Section, Row 8

George married Nancy S Dexter on 21 Nov 1844 in Dover-Foxcroft, Piscataquis, Maine. He became a Christian at the age of 15 and joined the church. He was ordained about 1860 and license several years before. He was 12 years clerk of the Penobscot Yearly Meeting and preached at Milo and other places. He had an excellent mind and was a good scholar and for a time a student in the biblical school. His sermons were carefully prepared, were instructive, suggestive and plain. He was an acceptable preacher until his health failed. He was a radical supporter of reforms, but was a kind and accommodating person.

He was very efficient in the business affairs of the church. In him the churches and institutions of the denomination had a true friend and helper.

Rev Porter S Burbank
Birth:
Mar. 13, 1810
Newfield
York County
Maine, USA
Death:
Jul. 21, 1883
Limerick
York County
Maine
Burial:
Baptist Society Church Cemetery
Limerick
York County
Maine

Rev. Porter S. Burbank, was a bro. of Rev. Samuel Burbank, (1792-1845), and 3rd in family to enter the ministry, and son of Samuel Burbank, a native of Rowley, Mass., and Susanna (Graves) Burbank, of Brentwood, NH.

He graduated Dartmouth, College in 1832, but took 3 yrs of his course in Waterville, College, ME. He prepared for college at Limerick Academy and Parsonfield Seminary.

Self-reliance and courage were required in procuring his education. At age 16 he was employed as apprentice under Wm. Burr in the "Morning Star" printing office at Limerick, and helped set type for the first number of that paper.

During his three yrs apprenticeship he became possessed with an intense disire for an education.

While fitting himself to teach he felt the call to the ministry. He preached some while at Waterville College, and was licensed by Waterville Q.M., at Industry, ME, 1836.

During his active ministry he probably taught a score of high schools. He loved to teach but at the close of his 3 yrs as principal of Stafford Academy, NH, he longed for the active work of the ministry. He was ordained at a session of NH Yearly Meeting, June 13, 1840. He afterwards taught a few terms at Parsonfield Seminary. A call to take charge of Clinton Seminary, NY and Whitestown Seminary was declined.

He was corresponding seretary of the Education Society six consecutive yrs. He was frequently on its board, and often made chairman of committees on education at General Conference. He was one of the committee that compiled the *"Psalmody."*

He was heartily interested in Temperance and Anti-slavery causes and the benevolent causes of the denomination, especially, the "Morning Star," newspaper, with which he was corresponding editor from 1833-1866.

He held pastorates in Hampton, Deerfield, New Hampton, and Danville, NH and in West Buxton and Lemerick, ME.

His ministry was eminently successful' several efficient Free Baptist ministers were converted in revivals in churches he pastored.

At the close of his last pastorate at Danville, NH, he purchased a home in So. Parsonfield, ME, where he spent the last ten yrs of his life. He supplied the church there one year and preached occasionally afterward.

Almira Wescott Bullock
Birth:
1797, USA
Death:
Apr. 25, 1859
Maine,
Burial:
Forest Hill Cemetery
Bridgton
Cumberland County, Maine
Plot: Chap. 19

Wife of Andrew Cobb married 1st: Rev. Jeremiah Bullock. She was an ordained minister of the Free Will Baptist, and went with her first minister husband, and later, her second husband, Dea. Cobb. Her son, Wescott Bullock, was also a minister. It is written she was a successful and much loved speaker, a Christian in all areas of her life.

Jeremiah Bullock

Birth:
1797
Death:
Dec. 16, 1849
Maine
Burial:
Forest Hill Cemetery
Bridgton
Cumberland County, Maine
Plot: Chap. 19

An ordained Free Will Baptist minister.

Wescott Bullock

Birth:
Jul. 7, 1818
Limington
York County, Maine
Death:
1900
Burial:
Greenwood Cemetery
Biddeford
York County, Maine

He received his education in the common schools and at Parsonsfield Academy, and was a teacher in early life. He began to preach soon after he embraced religion in 1842. He was ordained in Aug. 1856, in Saco, ME, his mother preaching the sermon to a vast assembly of people in the town hall. He was of fine build, very distinctive voice, with both his father and mother's qualities intertwined. He preached in N.H. and Maine with good success, was loved and esteemed by many.

The twofold and wonderfully woven mantle of his parents had fallen on him; that part received from his father, coarse, hard twisted and substantial, proved a panoply of security amid the storms that sometimes gathered about the minister's pathway; that inherited from his saintly mother and dyed by her gentle spirit, was of soft and silken texture designed to keep the heart warm and tender. This sacred mantel was "reversible" and sometimes changed in the pulpit, alternating between the rough and silken sides. He was ordained at Saco, in August 1856, preaching the sermon to a vast assembly of people in the town hall. He says "I have preached in various towns of Maine and New Hampshire, sometimes in a fine pulpit, sometimes in school house and sometimes standing on stone walls; wherever I had a thus saith the Lord." He has always preached what he believed and lived as he preached. In personal appearance both commanding and attractive; his voice pleasant and melodious, and his language plain and pure. He has been a very useful man, who was widely known and much beloved; now passing the snowy years of venerable age, cheered by the sunshine of the Christian's undying hope. He has been incapacitated for active service from paralysis, and says he "lives by praying"; resides in Biddeford, Maine. Indicates Ord. 1856. Son of Jeremiah Almira (Wescott) Bullock..

Asa Burnham
Birth:
Aug. 9, 1789
New Hampshire
Death:
Aug. 9, 1852
Garland, Maine
Burial:
Sebec Corner Cemetery
Sebec Piscataquis County, Maine

He was ordained, 1819 and pastored in Maine.

Inscription:
LIVERMORE
(back)
Rev. Asa Burnham
Died Aug. 9, 1852 Æ 63.
Hannah
His wife, died
May 14, 1887 Æ 99.

Oliver Butler
Birth:
Feb. 25, 1809
Berwick, York County Maine
Death:
Dec. 6, 1897
Chelsea,
Suffolk County,
Massachusetts
Burial:
Woodlawn Cemetery,
Biddeford,
York County, Maine

A graduate of Bowdoin College and for year's publisher of the "Biddeford Journal," a member of the Maine Legislature, two yrs president of the Senate, and at present (1889) attorney at law in Boston, Mass. Rev. Oliver Butler studied with a tutor and at Parsonfield Seminary in theology in 1843. He was licensed in June 1840 and ordained Jan. 28, 1842 a Free Will Baptist clergyman at Great Falls, N.H., by a council from the Rockingham Q.M., with Rev. Silas Curtis as Chairman. His first pastorate was at Effingham Falls where he organized a church and built a meeting house, adding during fourteen years, about 100 to the membership. He pastored Middleton, Wolsbourough, East Andover and at Parker's Head, ME, and for twelve years at Meredith Centre, N.H., where a hundred were baptized. He also pastored at Buxton, and Lyman, Me. He went into the publishing business in 1872, but continued preaching until 1880. When enfeebled by disease he moved to Chelsea, Mass, where he has served three yrs in a Baptist city mission. At nearly 80 years, he retired active service. He was three years a member of the Home Mission Board, and a member of Gen. Conference at Sutton, VT, in 1847, and Lowell, MA in 1852.

John Buzzell
Birth:
Sep. 16, 1767
Barrington, Strafford Cty
New Hampshire,
Death:
Mar. 29, 1863
Parsonsfield,
York County,
Maine
Burial:
North Parsonsfield
North Parsonsfield,
York County
Maine

Rev. John Buzzell, a Free Will Baptist clergyman, married Anna Buzzell, b. 1770, d. 1839. They had 11 children. His attainments were above average, early becoming a teacher of common schools. He

along with Dr. Moses Sweat, and Rev. Rufus McIntire, founded the Old Parsonsfield Seminary, the first school in the denomination.

He, with Elder Benjamin Randall founder of FWB in NH, came to Maine before 1800, and he is known to have pastored churches in Maine for more than 50 years. He was a noted and powerful preacher, dignified in his demeanor, yet in spirit humble. He did as much as any in extending the work and influence of the FWB church. It was said that he also had a talent for painting, 'as good as the old masters' and even painted a portrait of a young couple a week after their marriage as a gift to them. He had a far-reaching view of education, and had a commanding influence in exerting and molding political and religious opinions of the people. He was first editor of his denomination's "Morning Star" paper, which position he held seven years;

He was instrumental in establishing the Orissa Mission (India.) He wrote a biography of his mentor, *"Life of Rev. Benjamin Randall."* He died at his home in North Parsonsfield at the advanced age of ninety-five years, and 6 months.

Cyrus Campbell
Birth:
Sep. 29, 1817
Bowdoin
Sagadahoc County, Maine
Death:
Jun. 13, 1893
New Sharon
Franklin County, Maine
Burial:
Weeks Mills Cemetery
New Sharon
Franklin County, Maine

He was converted 25 years of age. He was a student of Whitestown, New York. On October 7, 1846 at the age of 29, he received license to preach and was ordained the following year in September. He pastored a number of churches in the area. On December 8, 1846 he married Adaline Lenpest.

Joseph Chadbourne
Birth:
Jun. 28, 1807
Greene
Androscoggin County, Maine
Death:
Nov. 20, 1877
Bradford
Penobscot County, Maine
Burial:
Corner Cemetery
Bradford, Penobscot County
Maine

Joseph Chadbourne, at the age of nineteen, while a student in the Seminary at Kent's Hill, became a Christian. Ten years afterwards he became a member of the church in Bradford. He was for a time the efficient deacon of the church. In 1858 he took a letter and joined the Christian denomination, by which he was ordained March, 1859. He was highly esteemed among them. Four years before his death, he again became a member of the church in Bradford. He was much interested in education and a successful teacher. He was frequently elected to officesof trust and responsibility.

Inscription:
JOSEPH CHADBOURNE died
November 20, 1877
Age 70 years   4 months   22 days

Edward R. Chadwick

Birth:
Jun., 1861
China
Kennebec County, Maine
Death:
1926
Burial:
Chadwick Hill Cemetery
China
Kennebec County, Maine

He was converted in 1878 and later graduated at the Maine Central Institute in 1880 and then from Bates College in 1884. He was of the class of 1888 of the Cobb Divinity School. In July, 1888 he settled in Milton, New Hampshire and on August 23 he was ordained by the New Durham Quarterly Meeting. His parents were: Abner D. Chadwick (1831-1911) and Drusilla Newcomb Chadwick (1836 - 1920)

Rev S. Freeman Chaney

Birth:
1819
Death:
Oct. 13, 1843
Burial:
Hillcrest Cemetery
West Buxton
York County
Maine

Oren Burbank Cheney

Birth:
Dec. 12, 1816
Ashland, Grafton County,
New Hampshire
Death:
Dec. 22, 1903
Lewiston,
Androscoggin County, Maine
Burial:
Riverside Cemetery, Lewiston,
Androscoggin County, Maine

Dr. Cheney attended Parsonfield Seminary and New Hampton Institution, and graduated from Dartmouth College in 1839. He was converted in the spring of 1836 and, walking from Dartmouth to his native place, he was baptized by Rev. Simeon Dana, and united with the Ashland church. After graduation he became principal of the Farmington ME Academy in the autumn of 1839. He became principal of the Strafford Academy in 1841. Then he taught the Greenland, N.H., and Academy near Portsmouth and was licensed by the Portsmouth church. He was ordained in the Effingham Hill, N.H. church, in the autumn of 1844, by Rev. John Buzzell, Rev. Benj. S.

Manson, and others. He held anti-slavery sentiments, and this pastorate was laid down because of opposition to his views. In 1851-52, he was sent to the Legislature by the Whigs and Free-soilers, and voted for the original Maine Temperance Law. In 1852, he went to Augusta for five years as pastor of the church. On Sept. 22, 1854, he received a letter from Rev. J. A. Lowell, principal of Parsonfield Seminary, announcing that the Seminary building had been burned the day before. From that day Dr. Cheney consecrated himself to build for the Free Baptists an efficient literary institution in a more central place. President Cheney held many important positions of confidence and trust in this denomination. Twice was moderator of General Conference, and occupied important position on the Conference Board. He represented his denomination as delegate to the General Baptists of England. He has been recording secretary of both the Foreign and Home Mission Societies, and president of the Education and Anti-Slavery Societies. He was foremost in vision to merge the Free Baptists with the larger open-communion Baptist, and worked to that end not only with Baptists but with Christian and other denominations until his demise. He is best known for being the founder and first president of Bates College in Lewiston, Maine. The college was chartered in 1862 and was founded as the Maine State Seminary in 1855.

Hubbard Chandler
Birth:
Jan., 1798
Death:
Nov. 5, 1866
West Poland,
Androscoggin County,
Maine
Burial:
Highland Cemetery,
West Poland,
Androscoggin County,
Maine

Rev. Chandler was converted and baptized before age 20 by his mother's brother, Rev. Jeremy Bean. He then began to preach and connected himself with the Second Wilton church, preaching in all the towns around and doing evangelistic work, holding revivals with great success. He was ordained at Phillips, ME, June 9, 1822, by Rev's Samuel Hutchins and John Foster. His travels as an evangelist in Maine extended to 120 towns and plantations. All the while, he supported himself, not receiving $50 a year for his labors. Though he was not favored with an extensive education, yet, he was gifted by nature. He was very conversant with Scripture. As a speaker, he was dramatic and was mighty in persuasive powers to move sinners. His earnestness and consecration enabled him to accomplish a great work. He raised up quite a number of churches in the new settlements he visited.

George Colby Dyer Chase
Birth:
Mar. 15, 1844
Death:
May 27, 1919
Burial:
Pond Cemetery 1,Unity,
Waldo County, Maine,
Plot: row 22

Blessed *are* the dead which die in the Lord

Professor of Rhetoric and English Literature in Bates College, Lewiston, Me., was born in Unity, Me. He prepared for college at the Maine State Seminary (afterwards Bates College), and immediately, entered Bates College, where he graduated in 1868.The next two years he was teacher of Greek, Latin and Mental Philosophy, at New Hampton Institution, N.H.
He then spent a year in Bates Theological School, and was at the same time a tutor of Greek in the college. He was at this time elected a professor in the college, and after

taking a post-graduate course of one year at Harvard College, entered upon the work of the professorship. He was a member of the Lewiston School Board and twice chosen. President in 1883 and 1887. In 1894 George Colby Chase, Class of 1868, succeeded President Cheney. Known as "the great builder," He oversaw the construction of eleven new buildings, including Coram Library, the Chapel, Chase Hall, Carnegie Science Hall, and Rand Hall. Chase tripled the number of students and faculty, and the endowment. He discontinued the Cobb Divinity School and Nichols Latin School departments of the College. In 1907 at the request of Chase and the Board, the legislature amended the college's charter removing the requirement for the President and majority of the trustees to be Free Will Baptists; this change to a non-sectarian status allowed the school to qualify for Carnegie Foundation funding for professor pensions He was for several years a contributor to the *"Morning Star."*

Uriah Chase
Birth:
Sept. 28, 1810
Death:
Aug. 1, 1888
Waterboro, Maine
Burial:
Elder Grey Cemetery
Waterboro
York County, Maine

He began to preach in 1848; licensed by the New Durham QM 1848; ordained at East Parsonfield, Me., 1850. All of his ministry was in Maine.

Rev Roger W Churchill
Birth:
Jul. 30, 1847
Shapleigh
York County
Maine
Death:
1914
Burial:
Mount Auburn Cemetery
Auburn
Androscoggin County
Maine

Rev. Roger W. Churchill, son of Nathaniel and Abigail W. (Stevens) Churchill, was born at Shapleigh,

ME, Aug. 30, 1848. He first studied for the law. He studied theology at Bates Theological School, and was converted in 1869, licensed in 1881, and was ordained in 1883, at Richmond, ME. He labored successfully there five years; he had two rivivals; sixty-four were added to the church. He is settled at Belmont, NH, where in one year twelve have been added. He married Maggie A. Archibald, Dec. 13, 1883, and has one daughter.

He was a brother to Edgar W. Churchill, 1858-1929, also a clergyman, per New Hampshire death records.

Aaron Clark
Birth:
Unknown
Death:
Dec. 11, 1880
Hennon, Maine
Burial:
Light Cemetery
Knox County, Maine,

He was converted at the age of thirteen. When seventeen years of age, he was licensed by the Methodists as an exhorter. He afterwards united with the Free Baptists, by whom he was ordained about 1840. He preached in several places within the limits of the Montville Q. M. His name appears in the Register in connection with the Washington church from 1848 to 1869; then as pastor of the Second Montville church till 1872; then as pastor of the Washington church till 1875; then as pastor of the South Montville church one year. He remained a member of the latter church till his death.

John Clark
Birth:
Unknown
Newcastle. Me.
Death:
Aug. 8, 1871
Prospect
Waldo County, Maine
Burial:
Clark Cemetery
Prospect, Waldo County, Maine

He married and moved to Monroe in early manhood, and in 1824, during a great revival in that section, he was converted and united with the church. He was licensed in1832, and ordained as an evangelist in 1838. He worked hard to support his family, and preached Sabbaths. He was in the ministry about forty years, and traveled in that time about forty thousand miles, at least one half of the distance on foot. He baptized

125, attended 100 funerals; and. Married sixty couples. He preached till within a few days of his death. Though born of poor parents and with limited education, his willing mind enabled him to do a good work Reverend John Clark for whom the Cemetery was named. He was a Veteran of the Battle of Hampden, War of 1812 and began the Clark Settlement, in Prospect, Maine. His broken gravestone is down and buried and no flag marks him as a veteran. He died at age 78 years 8 months, 19 days.

Death is the crown jewel for the Christian.

Jonathan Clay
Birth:
December 13, 1775
Buxton
Maine
Death:
Feb. 20, 1849
Maine
Burial:
Highland Cemetery
Buxton
York County, Maine

He was converted in 18 and five and was one of the early members of the Buxton church. He began to preach soon after his baptism and was ordained in 1815. His labors were mostly confined to Buxton and in 1831 he took his destination from his church and united with a few others who constituted a church near his home.

Rev Tisdale D. Clements
Birth:
Dec. 7, 1810
Monroe
Waldo County
Maine
Death:
Jul. 12, 1881
Burial:
Mount Rest Cemetery
Monroe
Waldo County,
Maine

Rev. T.D. Clements was ordained a Free Baptist minister in Maine; he was one of the first members of the Cooperation of Bates College, in Lewiston, and gave $1,000 to the endowment fund.

His death was noted in the 25th Gen. Conf. of Freewill Baptists list of ministers' deaths, since "last session of Gen. Conf. 1880.

Edward Lindley Cleveland
Birth:
Nov. 6, 1813
Camden
Knox County, Maine
Death:
Mar. 9, 1897
Rockport
Knox County, Maine
Burial:
West Rockport Cemetery
West Rockport
Knox County, Maine

He became a Christian at the age of 24 and was ordained in 1845 by Rev. John Hampton and others. He has preached an evangelist and labored in many revivals. He was a member of the Rockville Church, Camden, and preached as opportunity was offered him.

William G. Cobb
Birth
1779
Otisfield
Oxford Co., Maine
Death
Jun. 2, 1850

Otisfield
Oxford Co., Maine
Burial:
Cobb Hill Cemetery
Otisfield
Oxford Co. Maine

He was converted to at the age of 22 and was baptized by Rev. Zachariah Leach and after preaching considerably for 16 years was ordained in March, 1824. Ill health confined his labors near his home. Note: Age 70 yrs

Rev. Almira Wescott Cobb
Birth:
Oct. 2, 1795
Gorham
Cumberland County, Maine
Death:
Apr. 25, 1859
Maine
Burial:
Forest Hill Cemetery

Bridgton
Cumberland County, Maine
Plot: Chap. 19

She was the wife of Andrew Cobb Married 1st: Rev. Jeremiah Bullock 1797 - 1849) and mother of Rev. Wescott Bullock (1818 - 1900).

Greenleaf H Coburn
Birth:
Mar. 7, 1839
Turner
Androscoggin County, Maine
Death:
Jul. 11, 1865
Maine
Burial:
Gray Village Cemetery
Gray
Cumberland County, Maine

Died aged 26 years.He early showed a fondness for books. At fourteen he went to Boston, here he was employed till he was seventeen. He was converted in 1857, at Gray, ME, under the labors of Rev. W. T. Smith. He was baptized at once uniting with the church (Freewill Baptist) at Gray. In the spring of 1858, he returned to Boston for another year. Early in 1859, he went to Lewiston and entered Bates College, enjoying the love and esteem of his instructors, graduated from his preparatory course in July 1862. He then entered the Theological School at New Hampton (NH) and after three years graduated being ordained there July 17, 1865. A fortnight later he came to Lewiston and arranged with President

Cheney to enter the Junior Class of the College. But in two weeks he was dead from a fever. A gentleman offered to start him in business in Boston, and give him half the profits. "No," young Coburn replied. "I must get an education and enter upon a higher calling." President Oren B. Cheney, Bates College, preached his funeral sermon.

George Warren Colby
Birth:
Dec. 8, 1836
Vassalboro
Kennebec County, Maine
Death:
Jan. 22, 1913
Augusta
Kennebec County, Maine
Burial:
Mount Hope Cemetery
Augusta
Kennebec County, Maine

He was converted to the age of 23. He received license to preach from the Montville Quarter Meeting in March 1874 and was ordained on June 20, 1875 by Rev. Aaron Clark and others. In his many revivals he had between three and 400 conversion, baptized 73. Records show that he married 23 couples and attended 75 funerals.He married Ayrobine DAMON on 16 JAN 1879 in Vassalboro, Kennebec Cty, Maine.

Inscription:
COLBY /CONANT
George Warren Colby1836-1913

Joshua B. O. Colby
Birth:
Jan. 13, 1808
Maine
Death:
Mar. 27, 1891
Denmark
Oxford County, Maine
Burial:
Colby Cemetery
Denmark
Oxford County, Maine

He studied for a time at Fryeberg Academy. He became a Christian at the age the 26 and was baptized by Elder Jonathan Tracy and joined the church at Denmark. He was first ordained as a Deacon but soon after on October 6, 1852 was

ordained by Rev. James Rand and others. The church in Denmark was under his care for 40 years.
Inscription:
Rev. J. B. O. Colby
Born Jan. 13, 1808
Died Mar. 27, 1891

Jacob D. Couillard
Birth:
Nov. 24, 1815
Frankfort, Maine
Death:
Jul. 18, 1888
Maine
Burial:
Smith Cemetery
Palermo
Waldo County, Maine

He was converted in 1832, and an in Exeter, Maine was licensed in 1834. Two years later he was ordained. He had an itinerant ministry in which he baptized a good number of people and assisted in organizing several churches. After driving for some time in Massachusetts he moved to North Palermo, Maine and did a good work among the destitute churches. He also served during the Civil War.

Rev Gideon Cook
Birth:
Nov. 5, 1787
Eastham
Barnstable County
Massachusetts
Death: Dec. 7, 1869
Kennebunk
York County
Maine
Burial:
Pine Grove Cemetery
West Kennebunk
York County
Maine

Ordained Freewill Baptist minister   in   1826,   and ministered in Maine.

Inscription:
Rev. Gideon Cook Nov. 3, 1787 - Dec. 7, 1869

John Cook
Birth:
May 7, 1809
Alton, Belknap, New Hampshire
Death:
Jan. 4, 1891
Burnham, Waldo, Maine
Burial:
Burnham Village Cemetery
Burnham, Waldo County, Maine

His obituary appeared in the *Morning Star* published on 2 Apr

1891.Mary Jane (Adams) Cook married Rev. John Cook on 8 Nov 1846. His parents were Jacob and -- (Hubbard) Cook. His education he received from the common school Before he was sixteen his father moved on a new lot in Exeter, Me., where, in the midst of "black logs and flies," he was educated to work with his hands so effectively, that he could support himself and family' by working half the time and have the rest for preaching in destitute places without hire. He found a region of four towns without a preacher. In a town where there had been no religious meetings for ten years, he proclaimed the" glad tidings."He was converted at the age of twenty, received license to preach in 1833, and was ordained June 26, 1837, by Rev's Nathan Robinson, Roger Copp, and John B. Copp. He had revivals, baptized 141 converts in twelve different towns, assisted in organizing seven or eight churches, and married ninety-eight couples. He was chosen pastor of the Burnham church at its organization, July 2, 1857. During the war their church edifice was built. Though his pastorate ceased some time ago, he supplied the church from time to time,. He attended every monthly conference since 1860, and can tell how many times each member had been present for the last eighteen years. He was married Dec. 29, 1833, to Miss Sally P. Kenisten on Nov. 8, 1846, he was married again.

Lavina Carr Coombs
Birth:
Nov. 23, 1849
West Bowdoin
Sagadahoc County, Maine
Death:
1927
Burial:
Woodlawn Cemetery
West Bowdoin, Sagadahoc County,
Maine

Coombs, Miss Lavina C., daughter of David and Sarah Coombs, She commenced the Christian life in 1862; attended Litchfield Academy 1864-66, the Normal School at Farmington 187273, and the Lewiston High School in1880. She taught ten years in the schools of Maine, and in November, 1882, was sent by the Woman's Missionary Society as a missionary to India. She located at Midnapore, and took charge of the Zenana work and the Ragged Schools at that place. Was a Free Will Baptist missionary in India for forty years, teaching in a school and helping the team there. 1882- 1922.

He was converted to the age of 35 and send began to preach the gospel. He received his license on February 15, 1873 and was ordained by the Montville quarterly meeting on September 20, 1874. He pastored many of the churches in that area of Maine and held revivals throughout the region.He was a Member of Co.F 21st Me. Reg during the Civil War.

Roger Copp
Birth:
unknown
Death:
Feb. 16, 1860
Burial:
Detroit Village Cemetery
Detroit
Somerset County
Maine

A Freewill Baptist ordained minister, who pastored churches in Maine; his son, John B. and grandson, Prof. John Scott Copp, were also FWB ministers.

Rev David B. Cowell
Birth:
Dec. 20, 1807
West Lebanon, York County
Maine
Death:
Apr. 15, 1884
Maine
Burial:
Cowell-Corson
West Lebanon, York County
Maine

Freeman Cooper
Birth:
February 6, 1835
Wakefield, Maine
Death:
Apr. 11, 1900
Maine
Burial:
Oak Hill Cemetery
Windsor
Kennebec County, Maine

He studied in the Academy at Limerick, and also at Wolfborough, NH. He taught fifteen terms of school, mostly in his native town. His townsmen honored him with most of the offices in their power to bestow. He had an aptitude for mercantile pursuits, and at the age of seventeen began to keep a store in West Lebanon. After some years he went to Great Falls, where his trade became extensive. During this time he became a Universalist and then an infidel. But in 1833 he became clearly convinced of his error. Making his way through a crowded assembly, he stood upon the pulpit stairs and renounced his infidelity. He became a class leader in the Free Baptist church at Great Falls and an earnest worker. His conversation from house to house and over the counter was the means of many conversions. He soon felt called to preach, but was loth to give up his business. Finally, he yielded and first went to Barnstead, NH. He went then to Northwood, NH, North Berwick Me (Beach Ridge), Lebanon and Springvale. Others ministers baptized the converts during this time. In 1837, he was ordained. He traveled almost constantly for seven years and was associated in the ministry with Rev's Caverno, Thurston, Woodman, Place, Buzzell, Hobbs and others of the fathers. He was instrumental in the conversion of many, some of whom became ministers, and missionaries. In 1848 he suggested to Rev. O.B. Cheney, then pastor at West Lebanon, the idea of founding the Lebanon Academy and offered the land and one hundred dollars. One of his sons, educated in this flourishing school, became successful principal of Arms Academy, at Shelburne Falls, Mass. His last fields of labor were in Walnut Grove, N.H., a year or more, and six months in Gorham and Standish, ME.

In 1841, he married Miss Christiana B. Coffin, daughter of Rev. Stephen Coffin. She was talented, educated and zealous. She often accompanied him on his preaching tours, and aided him much, and in the Academy her influence on the students led many of them to Christ. Mr. Cowell was afflicted with heart disease many hears and kept close at home, but he was able to say, "It is alll clear now; the hope of other days sustains me still."

He and Christiana had three children: Hosea C. Cowell (1849 - 1853), Christiana M. Cowell (1853 - 1854), Eugene C. Cowell (1858 - **1862).**

Rev Simon Cox
Birth:
Apr. 14, 1800
Lincolnville
Waldo County
Maine
Death:
Jan. 28, 1851
Rockland
Knox County
Maine
Burial:
Achorn Cemetery
Rockland
Knox County
Maine

Rev. Simon Cox, died in Rockland, ME, aged 51 years. He was converted when about nineteen, and united with the Methodists, by whom he was licensed to preach. After about fifteen years, he united with the Free Baptists, and by them was recognized as an elder. While consumption was wasting his life, he was sustained by the gospel he preached to others."

He was married to Rachel Philbrook, with whom they had children: Deborah H. b. 1826; Aurelius Augustus, 1828; James Warren, 1829; Ruhama F. 1832; George Washington,1836; Hollis Monroe, 1837.

Charles T. D. Crockett

Birth:
Mar. 15, 1833
Woodstock
Oxford County,
Maine
Death:
Jun. 25, 1899
Maine
Burial:
Hunts Corner Cemetery
Albany
Oxford County,
Maine

He Was A Student At Gould's Academy In Bethel, Maine. After His Conversion On February 8, 1875 He Attended Bates Theological School, Lewiston, Maine. With his wife he was baptized at Mechanic Falls on May 16 1875 by Rev. B Menard. He was licensed to preach on January 27th,

1876 and ordained at Canton on June 8, 1877 by Rev. J. M. Pease, and others. He preached at West Paris where the church was revived and the next four years at Canton. After preaching at many churches in the area he settled at Jackson, New Hampshire where a house of worship was thoroughly repaired and well-furnished and the church strengthened by the addition of excellent members. In 1888 he became the pastor of the church at Steep Falls, Maine and served branched churches..

Their works do follow them.

True W. Dore

Birth:
Nov. 6, 1806
Death:
Mar. 26, 1879
Garland, Maine
Burial:
Hathaway Cemetery
Garland
Penobscot County, Maine

Converted in early man hood, he soon began to hold meetings. Gifted in prayer and song he labored as an evangelist with success. He first united with the Methodists, but it Ripley, Maine, he joined the Free Baptists and was ordained by them in June 1842. He preached at Ripley, Garland, and in the vicinity for other.

Inscription:
I have kept the faith.

Death is the entry to Life Evermore

Rev George Douglass
Birth:
Aug. 16, 1816
Bowdoin
Sagadahoc County, Maine
Death:
Aug. 25, 1845
Fairfield

Somerset County, Maine
Burial:
Litchfield Plains Cemetery
Litchfield Plains
Kennebec County, Maine

Rev. George Douglass experience religion at age twenty, was baptized in spring of 1836, and united with the church, and soon after began to preach. He was licensed in 1840 by the church, and was ordained in 1842 when he was engaged at Pittsfield, while engaged in a meeting there, by visiting ministers from the Waterville and Exeter Quarterly Meetings (QM). His work was blessed throughout the Waterville Q.M., in the addition of over one hundred within two years. He moved to Fairfield in 1843, and died there in the summer of 1845, in his 29th year.

Dr Daniel Dyer
Birth:
May 25, 1827
Charleston
Penobscot County
Maine
Death:
Oct. 2, 1892
Burial:

Mudgett Cemetery
Burnham
Waldo County
Maine
Plot: 14

His parents were Benjamin and Louisa (Sylvester) DYER. Converted at fourteen years of age, he studied at Litchfield Academy and at the Bowdoin Medical School, and has been successful as a physician.

He was licensed to preach in 1851, and afterwards ordained at North Anson. In 1852-53 he engaged in a revival to which over one hundred were converted. He has preached with needy churches. After three years' service his health failed.

He married in 1849 Miss Abby Weston.

Joseph Dyer
Birth:
1774
Boston
Suffolk County,
Massachusetts
Death:
Jan. 31, 1859
Phillips
Franklin County,
Maine
Burial:
Riverside Cemetery
Phillips
Franklin County
Maine

Rev. Joseph DYER, was the son of a sea-captain, and was one of the memorable party who threw the British tea into Boston harbor. His mother's was Elizabeth Nichols, of Malden, MA. At the age of eight years, Joseph's father died, and Joseph was bound out to learn the Morocco shoe trade. He married Miss Sally Merritt, of Malden, where he resided till he removed to Hallowell, ME, in October 1806. He had already experienced religion and joined the Calvinistic Baptist church in Massachusetts. He was ordained in 1810, and when the Free Baptist church which had been established by Benjamin Randall in 1795, was reorganized, Nov. 12, 1819, Rev. Dyer was one of the eleven included in the reorganization. With this church he was worthily connected until Sept. 17, 1831, when with others he organized a new church in Madrid, where his labors had been blessed. Over this flock he watched with ceaseless interest for more than a score of years, when failing health induced him to resign the charge to a younger brother.Though engaged in pioneer work in this section, making his way with his precious message on horseback through the wilderness, guided by spotted trees and preaching the gospel chiefly in log cabins, yet he was progressive and was practically interested in the moral and educational enterprises. He was devout and eminently spiritual in prayer. He lived to see his great-great-grandchild. He was universally esteemed.

Free From The Warfare

Ebenezer G Eaton
Birth:
Jul., 1808
Death:
Aug. 13, 1883
Lewiston, Me.
Burial:
Oak Hill Cemetery
Auburn,
Androscoggin County, Maine

Eaton died at age 76 years. He was thoroughly converted in1831. He studied at Parsonfield Seminary and held meetings in Freedom, N. H., where sixty were converted. He was ordained at Freedom July 14, 1833, by Rev's Hosea Quinby and John Buzzell. He was for a time a missionary in the Otisfield Q. M., being the first preacher in the Q. M. who received a salary. He preached in Otisfield, Harrison, Bridgton, Brunswick, Auburn, Buckfield, Canton, Livermore, Greene, Poland, South Lewiston, Bethel and Sabattus. He also preached three years in Nova Scotia, and in a great revival there one hundred and seventy-five were added to the churches. During his ministry, he baptized 1000 persons. He was a schoolmate of President Cheney, who wrote of Eaton, "He was a good man and full of the Holy Ghost and of faith, and much people was added unto the Lord."

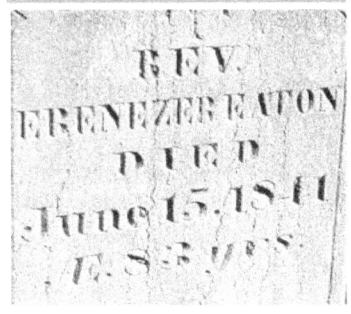

Ebenezer Eaton
Birth:
Unknown
Death:
Jun. 15, 1841
Androscoggin County, Maine
Burial:
Sedgwick Rural Cemetery
Sedgwick
Hancock County, Maine

Rev. Ebenezer Eaton Died June 15, 1841 (Age 83 years.). Ebenezer Eaton was the son of Theophilus Eaton and Abigail Fellows. He was married about 1777 to Abigail Herrick, the daughter of Joshua Herrick and Huldah Brown. Abigail is buried in Southwest Harbor, Maine, where Reverend Ebenezer Eaton was the town's first established minister. He was converted in 1831 after which he stated to attend Parsonfield Seminary and held meetings in Freedom, New Hampshire, where 60 were converted. He was ordained at Freedom on July 14, 1833, by Rev. Hosea Quinby and John Buzzell. He was for a time a missionary in the Otisfield Quarterly Meeting being the first preacher in the quarter meeting who received a salary. He preached in the churches at the following towns of Otisfield, Harrison, Bridgton, Auburn, and numerous other places in the area. He also preached three years in Nova Scotia and in the and in a great revival where 175 were added to the churches during his ministry he baptized 1000 people. He was a schoolmate of Pres. Cheney, who wrote of him, "he was a good man and full of the Holy Ghost and of faith, and much people were added unto the Lord.

Rev John Farnham
Birth:
1784
Death:
Oct. 6, 1847
Burial:
Woodside Cemetery
Belgrade
Kennebec County,
Maine

Ordained 1826, Freewill Bapt. minister. Labored in Maine.(Free Bapt. Cyclopedia, pub. 1889).

Death Is The Setting Free From The Warfare Of The Soul

Josiah Farwell
Birth:
Unknown
Death:
Mar. 10, 1872
Burial:
Pittsfield Village Cemetery,
Pittsfield,
Somerset County, Maine

Ordained a Free Will Baptist minister in 1817 in Maine, but after a time he left the church.

Rev Ebenezer Nichols Fernald
Birth:
Mar. 10, 1833
West Lebanon
York County
Maine
Death:
Jan. 15, 1898
Acton
York County
Maine

Burial:
Joseph Fernald Cemetery
Lebanon
York County
Maine

"Rev. Ebenezer N. FERNALD, was the son of Joseph and Polly (Nichols) Fernald. He was converted in 1842. He was fitted for college at New Hampton, NH, from 1855-58. In Aug. 1858, he entered Amherst College (MA) and graduated in 1862. After teaching four years he entered Andover Theological Seminary, and graduated in 1869. He was licensed to preach in 1868, and ordained by a council of the Boston Quarterly Meeting (QM) in Dec. 1869. He was pastor of a church which he organized at Winthrop, Mass, from 1868 to 1870. From 1870-1874, he was pastor of the church in Auburn, Maine. The next two years he was corresponding secretary of the Education Society. From 1876 to 1883 he was financial secretary of the Home Mission, Foreign Mission, and Education Societies [Freewill Baptist], and treasurer of the same societies until 1885.

He then became publisher of "The Morning Star.

He was married Dec. 27, 1863, to Miss Anna B. Tuxbury. Two of their five children are living. Mrs. Fernald has been for some years a member of the board of managers of the Woman's Missionary Society.

preached with this church, or in an adjacent town, for thirty years. He was mild in his address yet firm and unflinching for the truth. His upright life won for him a large circle of friends. Having suffered from feeble health for years, he went from work to reward.

Rev Allen Files
Birth:
1791
Gorham
Cumberland County, Maine
Death:
Mar. 20, 1864
Benton, Maine
Burial:
Grover Cemetery
Woolwich
Sagadahoc County, Maine

He was born in Gorham. Me., in 1791, where he was converted, and soon entered upon an itinerant ministry, in which many mere converted. In 1819, the revival in Lincolnville, under his labors, continued until a hundred accepted Christ. He was then ordained. In 1823, with Rev. J. M. Bailey, in Woolwich, he saw more than a hundred converted. In the extensive revival in Richmond, in 1825, he, with Rev. Clement Phinney, led a hundred to the Saviour. He became pastor for five years at Topsham, ME. He married about this time Miss Susan Shaw, of Woolwich, and purchasing a small farm, moved to Wales, and united with the church there. He

Charles W. Foster
Birth:
Feb. 3, 1836
Harrison, Maine
Death:
Sep. 16, 1902
Burial:
Evergreen Cemetery
Phillips
Franklin County,Maine

He attended the Bridgeton Academy and Westbrook Seminary. He was converted on May 30, 1870 in the Methodist Church at South Harrison. After three years he yielded to a call to the ministry and preached his first sermon in the Grand Hill schoolhouse in York. He was licensed in 1874 and ordained by the York and Cumberland Christian conference on October 19, 1875. On June 21, 1878 he united with the Free Baptist Church in Bridgeton. He was also treasurer of the town of Bridgeton for three years. In the Civil War he served in Battery A 1st. Reg. Me. Vol. Lt. Art._Regt.

Rev Thomas Flanders
Birth:
1780
Alton, New Hampshire
Death:
1889
Burial:
Knowlton Mills Cemetery
Piscataquis County, Maine

Ordained 1825. Itinerated in Maine and New Hampshire.

Rev Jabez Fletcher
Birth:
Jul. 2, 1800
Gray
Cumberland County, Maine
Death:
May 13, 1878
Dixmont
Penobscot County, Maine
Burial:
Simpson's Corner Cemetery
Dixmont
Penobscot County, Maine

Rev. Jabez Fletcher at age 24 was converted, and after about three years, he began to hold meetings. He was ordained by the Freewill Baptist at the June session of the Prospect Quarterly Meeting (QM), in 1833, at Dixmont. His early ministry was blessed in Dixmont, Prospect, Waldo, Monroe, Brooks and on the islands of the coast. He was an advocate of all moral enterprises and a man of excellent spirit.

Fletcher who more than 50 years ago, drove his ox-team from New Hampshire 160 miles to Dixmont, in Maine and cleared a farm there, toiling all the week and preaching without compensation on the Sabbath. He died after a long and useful life, aged 78 years.

Joseph Foss
Birth:
1765
Lee,
Strafford County,
New Hampshire,
Death:
Dec. 28, 1852
Brighton,
Somerset County, Maine
Burial:
Mount Rest Cemetery,
Athens,
Somerset County,
Maine

An ordained Free Will Baptist minister. He went west to Brighton, ME, in 1812, and began holding meetings. He became pastor there and stayed pastor for forty years, doing much ministerial work in towns that had no regular minister. He preached more than fifty years and died in his 88th year of age.

William E. Foy
Birth:
1818
Death:
Nov. 9, 1893
Burial:
Birch Tree Cemetery
East Sullivan
Hancock County, Maine
Plot: Very back of the cemetery on the right

William was born a free black. His parents were Joseph and Betsy Foy. His home was near Augusta, Maine. Even though slavery was not tolerated in the north, free people of color were not considered equal to whites.

There isn't a lot of information about Foy's parents, but seems that Foy was allowed to read books and attend school. William Foy had a friend whose name was Silas Curtis. Silas was an ordained Freewill Baptist. It was through the ministry of Silas that Foy became converted at the age of 17. Foy continued to study and followed his mentor's footsteps in becoming a minister. Foy was an unusual black man. Foy was tall and light skinned. He was gifted as an eloquent speaker. Witnessing for God, however, wasn't always easy for Foy. He worked hard among both the blacks and whites and led many people to know Jesus. Early in 1842, Foy had experienced two visions about Christ's second coming and the reward of the righteous. Because of the visions, he joined the Millerite movement. However, he was reluctant to relate the visions publicly because he was aware of the prejudice displayed toward blacks. Foy was attending ministerial school in Boston at the time. A fellow pastor of the Episcopal Methodist Church encouraged Foy, and he began relating the visions to large audiences throughout New England.

The third and last vision Foy experienced was in 1844. That vision showed three levels. #1...God guiding his people from truth to truth; #2...testing the truths God's people had discovered; and #3...ultimate victory when the saved reach the Holy City because they believed and followed God's messages. Foy was experiencing financial pressures and there were things about the vision that he could not understand. Therefore, he stopped recounting them. Foy moved back to Maine and continued to minister to the FW Baptist and Methodist congregations. William Foy is considered as a prophet for the time prior to the Great Disappointment.

Inscription:
Rev. William E. Foy.
Died in Plantation at Age 74 years.
Also buried here is his daughter,
Laura, age 7 years

Rev Charles S. Frost
Birth:
1849
New Hampshire, USA
Death:
1933
Burial:
Laurel Hill Cemetery
Saco
York County
Maine

A Freewill Baptist minister, ordained 1878. A graduate of Bates College in 1874, and Bates Theological Seminary in 1878.

Jarius Fuller
Birth:
May 27, 1805
Maine
Death:
Jan. 23, 1877
Maine,
Burial:
Harding Cemetery
Brunswick,
Cumberland County,
Maine

Jarius married Sophia (Cargill) Fuller. He was an ordained minister/pastor in the Freewill Baptist church in Maine, and pastored in Greene, ME, where in 1826, revival was seen in that church, resulting "in twenty being added to the church." He also pastored at So. Monmouth, and other places, and was known to be a faithful man.

Rev Harold Ionel Frost
Birth:
Nov. 13, 1886
New Hampshire
Death:
Mar. 4, 1976
Auburn
Androscoggin County
Maine
Burial:
Mount Auburn Cemetery
Auburn
Androscoggin County
Maine

He was the son of Rev. Robert D. and Hattie (Parrott) Frost, born in 1886, in NH.

His father moved to different states going to school, pastoring, etc.

On this cemetery record, it gives the title, "Rev" with his name, and also shows his wife, Mabel's m/n. His WW I Draft Registration,[1918] states that he was a Missionary to India in 1917 for the American Baptist Foreign Mission [prev. to 1911, Free Baptist], and was on furlough from Balasore, Orissa, India, arriving in USA in 1918. He lived to the age of 89 years.

Rev Robert D. Frost
Birth: 1846
Monroe County
New York
Death: 1921
Cumberland County
Maine
Burial:
Bay View Cemetery
South Portland Gardens
Cumberland County
Maine
Plot: Sec. 7 Lot 24

Rev. Robert D. Frost received license to preach in Iowa, 1866. He graduated from the Cedar Valley Seminary, Osage, IA in 1871, from Hillsdale College, Mich. in 1873 and from Bates Theological School, Lewiston, ME in 1881. Upon graduation, he was accepted as a missionary to India, and was ordained at Dover, NH in Feb. 1874, by the Freewill Baptist

Foreign Mission Society. He sailed for India March 18, and was located in Midnapore. He acquired the native language rapidly and soon engaged in bazar and itinerant preaching and supplied the Bhimpore station for a time.

In late 1875, he sent his resignation intending to start for America the next year, but by March 1, 1876, two ladies of the mission, disabled by sickness--one of them helpless-- were sent home, and with the advice of his colleagues he accompanied them. He was himself suffering with fever.

After his return, he preached in Limerick, ME, and then in 1877, he entered the Theological School, studying the original languages of the Bible and afterwards completed the progressive course of the Correspondence School of the American Institute of Hebrew.

He was married to Miss Hattie G. Parrott of Cape Elizabeth, ME, on Oct. 1, 1885. They have a son, bn Nov. 13, 1886. After about two years he, pastored churches in ME and NH, and beginning in Aug. 1877, he entered upon pastorate at Block Island, R.I.

He was delegate to General Conference in 1889.

He was a useful minister, pastor and theologian.

John Fullonton
Birth:
Aug. 8, 1812
Death:
Apr. 17, 1896
Burial:
Riverside Cemetery
Lewiston
Androscoggin County, Maine
Plot: 0605W

He graduated from Dartsmouth College, 1840. He was a teacher at Parsonfield, Whitestown Seminary and studied for the ministry at Whitestown Biblical School. He was ordained at Whitestown, Jan. 5, 1845. Then he became a professor of Hebrew and Church History, and after 1851 of Ecclesiastical History and Pastoral Theology at Whitestown Biblical School, 1850-4; New Hampton Theological Institution, 1854-77; and Bates Theological School, 1877-98. Delegate to the General Conference, 1847.Editor of The Dartmouth, 1839-40. Assistant Editor o the Morning Star 1839-98. D.D. from Dartmouth College, 1869.

William F Gallison
Birth:
Windham,
Me,
Jan. 14, 1799
Death:
Mar. 9, 1858
Burial:
Dover Cemetery,
Dover-Foxcroft,
Piscataquis County,
Maine,
Plot: North Section, Row 3

At age eighteen, he professed Christ, and was baptized by Rev. C. Phinney in Feb. 1817. He moved to eastern Maine at age twenty-five, and settled in Charlotte. He united with the Christian church in that place and maintained an outward life beyond reproach. He served his townsmen as officer in the militia and as magistrate. In 1832, he was a member of the State Legislature. In 1834, moving to Dover, Me, he joined the Free Will Baptist church, and the next year began his gospel ministry. He had in early life received a good academic education. He was licensed by the Sebec Quarterly Meeting, in January, 1840, and was ordained in Dover, July 8, 1841. His labors in the ministry were confined mostly to the Sebec Q.M. Fourteen ministers attended his funeral.

Rev Danville A Gammon
Birth:
Jul. 20, 1861
Canton, Maine
Death:
Dec. 26, 1910
Burial:
Roxbury Village Cemetery
Roxbury
Oxford County
Maine

Rev. Danville A. Gammon, son of Charles E. and Matilda T.(Brown) Gammon. He studied at Maine Central Institute. He was licensed to preach Dec. 9, 1886, and ordained Jan. 1, 1889. He was pastor of the Weld church from November, 1886 to April, 1888. He then became pastor of the Second Wilton and Chesterville churches. He married Carrie A. Locke, on May 6, 1891, in Maine.

Mark Gatchell
Birth:
May 17, 1812
Litchfield
Kennebec County Maine
Death:
Jul. 28, 1887
Burial:
Litchfield Plains Cemetery,
Litchfield Plains,
Kennebec County, Maine

He became a Christian under the labors of the Rev. Dexter Waterman and was baptized at the age of 16. He began to preach at the age of 20 and was licensed two years afterwards. He was ordained by a council at the Bowdoin Quarterly Meeting at 24 years of age. He pastored many churches in Maine and records show that he was asked 25 times to harmonize difficulties in churches. He was a member of the legislature the year that a grant was made to the Maine State Seminary.

Rev Benjamin S Gerry
Birth:
May, 1821
Freedom
Waldo County, Maine
Death:
Feb. 19, 1885
Dexter
Penobscot County, Maine
Burial:
Mount Pleasant Cemetery
Dexte, Penobscot County, Maine

He was born in Freedom, Waldo Co. ME, where he lived until six yrs of age, when his parents moved to Dover. He lived there until 1864 when he bought a farm near Dexter where he resided until his death.

In 1846, he married Miss Maranda Rowe, of South Dover, in whom he found a worth companion and helper. He was converted at the age of thirteen and baptized at the age of nineteen and united with the Methodists.

He afterwards, from doctrinal conviction, joined the Free Baptist church at South Dover, and later the West Sangerville church, of which he was pastor many years and a member at the time of his death. In 1853 he began to preach. He was ordained in 1858 at So. Dover, Rev. E. Harding preaching the sermon. His ministry was mostly within the limits of the Penobscot Yearly Meeting (Y.M.) and especially in the Exeter and Sebec Quarterly Meetings (Q.M.) and especially in the Exeter and Sebec Q.M's. He held pastorates in Corinth, First and Second Sangerville, Corinna, Bradford, LaGrange, Charleston, Abbott, Atkinson, and Ornesville. He also preached at Nmber Eight (Willimantic). Revival interests followed his labors and many were converted. He was deeply interested in missions, temperance and education, and a father in his Q.M. For twenty-one consecutive years he was its clerk, and during that time he was absent but once. He was a good and faithful man.

William Getchell
Birth:
Dec. 6, 1793
Vassalborough, Me.,
Death:
Oct. 30, 1867
Pittsfield, Me.
Burial:
Carr Cemetery
Pittsfield, Somerset County, Maine

He married, Aug. 22, 1814, Miss Mary Leavitt, of Clinton. In the summer of 1818 he was converted and united with the Christian church at East Pittsfield. In August, 1823, having moved to another part of Pittsfield, he was instrumental in organizing a Freewill Baptist church and was chosen one of its deacons. In September 1826 he was ordained by a council from the Exeter Q. M. as pastor of the church with which he was connected. This relation he held till death. He also acted as pastor of the Second Pittsfield church and of the Burnham church for over twenty years. He solemnized over one hundred and fifty marriages and attended hundreds of funerals.

Rev Orison L Gile
Birth:
Oct. 22, 1857
Bennington
Hillsborough County
New Hampshire
Death:
May 31, 1892
Burial:
Ridge Road Cemetery
Bowdoinham
Sagadahoc County
Maine

"Rev. Orison L. Gile, was the son of P.S.H. and Mary B. (Dodge) Gile, and was born in Bennington NH, Oct. 22, 1856. He became a Christian at the age of sixteen.

He prepared for college at New Hampton Institution, NH, from 1875-1878, graduated from Bates College, Lewiston, ME, in 1883, and from Bates Theological School in 1886. He received license to preach from the Weare Q.M., NH, Feb. 1880, and was ordained at Richmond, ME June 8, 1886, by

Rev's C.F. Penney, J.B. Jordan, A.B. Drew, R.W. Churchill, C.E. Cate and others.

He was pastor at Lisbon Falls during his course of study, also of the Pine Street church, Lewiston, two years. He has been instrumental in a large number of conversions and has received sixty-two persons into the churches. He was in 1887 pastor at Richmond Village, ME, and in 1888 at Cape Elizabeth.

He was married, Jan. 1, 1884, to Miss Linda E. NELSON, who died.

In June, 1887, he married Miss Sarah E. Libby, or Richmond Village."

He became a Christian at the age of 20. In 1860 he moved on Houlton, Maine, where he lived 16 years and then moved on to Amity where he resided for some time. He received license in 1868 and was ordained in the same year. His pastorates were at the Glenwood church, a Littleton, second Hodgdon, and other churches in that area of Maine. He had revivals in each of the churches where he pastored and baptized over 100 converts. He organized a Littleton and Haynesville churches.

Harry O Gidney
Birth:
July 9, 1829
Cambridge
New Brunswick
Canada
Death:
Nov. 11, 1895
Maine
Burial:
South Amity Cemetery
South Amity
Aroostook County, Maine

Capt Philip Gilkey, Sr
Birth:
Jan. 25, 1788
Islesboro
Waldo County, Maine
Death:
Jan. 5, 1872
Searsport
Waldo County, Maine
Burial:
Gordon Cemetery
Searsport, Waldo County, Maine

He lived in Isles borough till forty years of age, and the rest of his life in Searsport. He was converted in youth, but did not decide to preach till he was more than fifty years of age. He was then a Baptist. His first efforts were in the town of Eden, Mt. Desert, where some were converted. He was then ordained by the Free Baptists, and preached mostly in Eden. Philip was married to Jane Pendleton (1789 - 1821) They had 7 children. After Jane died, Philip married Deborah Cushing (1787 - 1865). They had 6 children. Deborah was the widow of Philip's brother Jacob. After Deborah died, Philip married Judith Pendleton (1794- 1892), they had no children.

Rev Arthur Given
Birth:
Feb. 27, 1841
Wales Corner

Androscoggin County, Maine
Death:
Feb. 22, 1925
Maine
Burial:
Riverside Cemetery
Lewiston
Androscoggin County Maine
Plot: 0267

His father bore the same name, and was a highly esteemed citizen, whose occupation was that of a farmer. Previous to the age of eighteen the son was employed part of the time on the farm, attended the district school, spent one term at the Litchfield Liberal Institute, and another at the Maine State Seminary at Lewiston.

At this age he was released from further service at home, and commenced his perparation for college at the last named institution. He secured the means to pay his expenses by teaching and manual labor. Subsequent to the completion of this preparatory course of study, in 1862, he served nine months in the army.

In the fall of 1863 he entered Bates College, and graduated in 1867 in a class of eight, the first graduating class of the college. He was its valedictorian.

He became at once principal of the New Hampton Literary Institution, and after a year of successful service, resigned, and was for two years principal of Maine State Seminary at Lewiston.

From 1870 to 1872 he was a student in the theological department of Bates College, and during part of the time was a tutor in the college.

In September, 1872, he became pastor of the Essex Street church at Bangor, and was ordained in the December following by the Unity Quarterly Meeting. He continued in this relation until March, 1875, when he became pastor of the church at Greenville, R.I. In February, 1881, he resigned this position to become the joint pastor of the church at Auburn and of a mission of the Rogers Williams church at Arlington. In 1883 he relinquished Arlington, and in 1885 he resigned his Auburn parish to become general treasurer of the benevolent societies of the denomination. During his pastorate at Auburn there was begun the erection of a large and commodious house of worship which was dedicated early in 1889. Since 1873 he has been one of the board of overseers of Bates College, and in 1880 was chosen its secretary. For several years he has been a member of the executive board of the Education Society, and 1880-85 its corresponding secretary. He was till 1885 the secretary of the Rhode Island Sunday-School Union, and for several years clerk of the Rhode Island Association. In July, 1889 he was elected a corporator of the "Star."

He married Dec. 22, 1868, Miss Lura Durgin, sister to Mrs. John Malvern, of Sanbornton, N.H., and has one daughter.

He had a brother, Rev. Lincoln Given, b. 1827, who was a teacher/minister to Maine Freewill Baptist churches.

Lincoln Given
Birth:
Nov. 7, 1827
Wells, Maine
Death:
Oct. 8, 1894
Maine
Burial:
Pond Road Cemetery
Androscoggin County
Maine

He was a brother of the Arthur Given. He was converted at the age of 15 and was baptized by Rev. E. J. Eaton and United with the church in Wales in the spring of 1843. He received his early education at Litchfield Institute, and his theological in the Biblical School at New Hampton. In June 1854 he received license to preach from the Bowdoin Quarterly Meeting and in June 19,1859 he was ordained at a session of the Springfield Quarter Meeting At Weston by Rev. L. M. Hagget and others. Most of his pastorates was in Maine and New Hampshire. However he did spend 18 months in Minnesota and six months in Illinois where many were converted for his efforts. He was a member of the General Conference three different times. He taught 15 terms of school and served as a supervisor 15 years. In 1851 he married Miss Lucy A. Colby who died in 1869 and afterwards he married in December 1873 Miss Carrie Weymount.

Rev Cleaveland B Glidden
Birth:
Sep. 28, 1822
Woolwich
Sagadahoc County,
Maine
Death:
May 15, 1864
Gardiner
Kennebec County,
Maine
Burial:
South Gardiner Cemetery
South Gardiner
Kennebec County,
Maine

Rev. Cleaveland B. Glidden, died after an illness of three days in Gardiner, ME, May 15, 1864. He was born in Woolwich, ME, Sept. 28, 1821(sic). At sixteen he was converted, baptized by Rev. C. Quinnam and united with the church in his native place. After a struggle he yielded to God and began his ministry. He was ordained in Gardiner, July 5, 1855, and settled with the First church there. He was also pastor at West Gardiner, Jefferson, Whitefield, and five years of the Monmouth church.

His funeral services were conducted by Rev. J. Mariner in the meeting-house at South Gardiner. He was an upright Christian and a humble, devoted minister of the gospel.

Joseph Goodwin
Birth:
Jul. 10, 1788
Death:
Mar. 21, 1850
Wells, Maine
Burial:
Goodwin Cemetery
Oxford County, Maine

Barnard Goodrich
Birth:
1800
Nottingham, N. H.
Death:
Mar. 20, 1883
Burial:
Ripp Cemetery
West Gardiner
Kennebec County, Maine

He became a Christian in early life. About 1831 he moved to Maine. He preached and baptized in Monmouth, West Gardiner, Greene, Litchfield, South Gardiner and Richmond. He supported himself at the trade of blacksmith and preached as opportunity Offered.

He was converted in 1801, and on August 28 joined the Baptist church. The next year his name appears as one of the committee who transcribed the articles of faith and records of this newly organized church. Later difficulties some years distracted the church and the radical preaching of the election by the pastor caused some to question the doctrine. He and 13 others were expelled on June 4, 1807. They associated themselves for worship with himself as the leader. In 1808 a revival followed and a Free Baptist church was organized over which he was ordained as pastor in 1812 and for 13 years this relationship existed. He supported his family by labor in the ship-yards but his excellent gift of exhortation frequently gave him wholely to the Lord's work.

Oh! How precious is the dust of a believer!

Spouses: Abigail Penny Gowell (_____ - 1845), Prudence Moulton Gowell (_____ - 1886)*

Inscription:
75 years 8 months 26 days

Rev William Gowell
Birth:
Mar. 6, 1808
Androscoggin County
Maine
Death:
Jan. 1, 1884
Poland
Androscoggin County
Maine
Burial:
Mount Auburn Cemetery
Auburn
Androscoggin County
Maine

John Grant
Birth:
Unknown
Death:
Oct. 25, 1882
Bucksport
Hancock County,
Maine
Burial:
Oak Hill Cemetery
Bucksport
Hancock County, Maine

He was a native of the Province of New Brunswick, but moved to Maine in 1839. He was converted to the age of 16 and publicly professed Christ eight years later and in 1842 was baptized uniting with the Hodgdon church. He was licensed by this church in 1859 and ordained a few years later. His preaching was characterized by interesting expositions of Scripture.

Andrew Gray
Birth:
Sep. 2, 1823
Brooksville, Maine
Death:
Mar. 24, 1901
Burial:
Otter Creek Cemetery
Hancock County, Maine

He was converted at the age of 28, and was licensed to preach on December 12, 1854 and ordained on June 17, 1872. He had for pastors and baptize 83 converts at four churches.

Stephen Gross
Birth:
unknown
Death:
Nov. 27, 1887
East Bucksport
Hancock County, Maine
Burial:
Granite Cemetery
Orland
Hancock County, Maine

He died at age 85 and his wife only two days later. Throughout his earnest early ministry many of the churches in the Ellsworth Quarterly meeting were strengthened, if not planning. He was loyal to his denomination and an early subscriber and devoted reader of *The Morning Star*. He was earnest in securing the salvation and especialty of the young, and in urging them to seek good learning as an advantage for their life work. **Throughout his faithfulness many found their saviour.**

S. M. Haggett
Birth:
Nov. 8, 1818
Edgecomb
Lincoln County, Maine
Death:
Aug. 23, 1878
Springfield
Penobscot County, Maine
Burial:
Mills Cemetery
Springfield, Penobscot County, Maine

At the age of seventeen he became a Christian and united with the church in his native town. Soon he felt called to the ministry, and received encouragement from the church.In 1840, he went to Parsonfield Seminary, and was a student there three years. The Edgecomb Q.M. gave him license in 1842. He traveled and preached in New Hampshire and Vermont with good success. From 1845 to 1849, he preached in Penobscot. In 1849 he settled at Monroe. The next year, in June, he was ordained by the Prospect Quarterly Meeting. After several years at Monroe he went to North Bangor, where many were converted under his labors. At this place in 1852, he married Miss Delia H. Rollin.The next year he preached in the Springfield Q.M. At Chester he held meetings and where he organized a church. He was a delegate to General Conference in 1856. The same year he became pastor of the Springfield church. He served as clerk of the Q.M. sixteen years and attended all its sessions and all the Yearly Meetings. He was the town clerk nine years. In 1871, he resigned the pastorate of the Springfield and Carroll church, and in 1873 he served as missionary in the Springfield Q.M. The next two years he preached in Gardiner, ME, and then returned to Springfield. He baptized over four hundred, and attended over eight hundred funerals.

Rev Turner Hanson
Birth:
May 27, 1810
Death:
Apr. 3, 1876
Burial:
Saint Albans Village Cemetery
Saint Albans
Somerset County
Maine

An ordained Free Baptist minister in Maine, whose death was in the list of names of ministers who had died. He was listed as being from St. Albans.

of 14 churches and had revivals in 15. He baptized over 150 people. He organized eight churches during his ministry. Five times he was a delegate to the General Conference and wants to the Free Christian Baptist Conference of New Brunswick.

Ephraim Harding
Birth:
December 23, 1809
New Sharon, Maine
Death:
1892
Burial:
Corinthian Cemetery
Corinth
Penobscot County, Maine
Plot: Div. 3 Lot 25

His father was Jedediah Harding M.D.who was buried at sea when Ephraim was only 13 months old. At the age of seven he was sent away on among strangers. He was converted on October 25, 1825, at the age of 13 and was baptized by Rev. Samuel Hutchins, united with the church in his native town. In 1838, he began to preach and on October 13 received his license. January 29, 1843, he was ordained at New Portland by the Anson Quarterly Meeting. He was pastor

Lot L Harmon

Birth:
1826
Madison, New Hampshire
Death:
1905
Burial:
Mount Auburn Cemetery
Auburn
Androscoggin County, Maine

He became a Christian when 10 years old and studied at Parsonsfield Seminary and Bangor Theological Seminary. He was licensed in 1856, and was ordained March 5, 1857 by Rev's. M.J. Steere, P. S. Burbank and J. R. Cook. He pastored churches throughout the area and after graduating from the Seminary he continued to pastor the North Bangor church and made a specialty of Sunday school work, mostly in Maine. Being a gifted musician and singer, sometimes for weeks he talked and sang with the children three or 3 1/2 hours a day. He was a member of the Maine legislature in 1866 and assisted in getting the charter of the Maine Central Institute. He was a general agent of the Sunday School Union from 1868 to 1883 and recording Sec. of Free Baptist Sunday School Union from 1877 to 1882. Before he entered the ministry he was a justice of the peace and had charge of schools in Madison, New Hampshire.

Ephraim H. Hart

Birth:
June 11,1809
Death:
Jan. 4, 1877
Lynn, Mass.
Burial:
Hiram Village Cemetery
Hiram
Oxford County
Maine

He studied at Parsonsfield Seminary and Strafford Academy. He was licensed in 1838 and ordained at Brownfield, Me. Dec. 23, 1840. Most of his ministry was in Maine. Spouse: Frances B. Hart (1815 - 1897)

Samuel Hathorn
Birth:
Sep. 14, 1794
Bowdoinham
Sagadahoc County,
Maine
Death:
Dec. 13, 1858
West Gardiner
Kennebec County,
Maine
Burial:
Ridge Road Cemetery
Bowdoinham
Sagadahoc County,
Maine

Rev. Samuel Hathorn was converted in 1817 in revival conducted by Asa Foster. He was active and consecrated, and 1819, in connection with Andrew Rollins and one other, he purchased a tract of land and began clearing it. In Jan. 1821, Rollins began to preach, and Hathorn soon sold the land and began his labors with the Rock River church in the vicinity in Sept. 1825. The First Church in town grew from this church. He was licensed by the Bowdoinham Quarterly Meeting, in Oct 1825, and Jan. 12, 1826 was ordained. After an itinerant ministry of five or six years in his QM, he extended labors over the state. Late in 1836 he went to Indiana and after a brief visit to Maine in the summer of 1837, he returned and settled at Milan, Ripley Co. Indiana with his wife, and lived there three years. Finding the climate ill suited to their health, they returned to the home of their early years. Before 1844, he had made four tours through the Western States. In 1852, his wife died of consumption. In July 1853 he married Cordelia Clough, who survived him. They spent the following winter in the Western States and on their return to Maine they purchased a farm at West Gardiner. He preached his last sermon May 30, 1858 at Bowdoinham Ridge from Hosea 6:3. He spoke of his uninterrupted peace and joy, and of the brightness of his hope beyond. During his ministry he baptized 1350 persons. Many churches were gathered and organized.

George W Haskell
Birth:
Dec.9, 1814.
Poland,ME.
Death:
Dec. 31, 1874
Hodgdon, Aroostook County, Me.

Burial:
Hodgdon Cemetery
Hodgdon,
Aroostook County, Maine

He became a Christian in early life, and resisted for some time a call from God to the ministry. He was ordained in 1840, and after three years of very successful evangelistic work, moved to Aroostook County. In 1844 he married Miss Hannah M. Smith, of Hodgdon, and resided in the town of Hodgdon the remainder of his life. His labors in Aroostook County were very extensive, and resulted in the conversion of about one thousand, the most of whom he baptized. His last work for the Master was the erection of the house of worship at Hodgdon. He identified himself with the anti-slavery movement, and represented his district in the Legislature in 1855, 1866, and 1867. As the result of his benevolence and large heartedness, he had great popularity.

Inscription:
In Memory of
Rev George W Haskell
Died Dec. 31, 1874 AE 60 yrs
He being dead yet speaketh

Asa Hathaway
Birth:
Sep. 26, 1842
Atkinson, Maine
Death:
Apr. 20, 1914
Burial:
Hathaway Cemetery
Garland
Penobscot County, Maine

He was educated in the public schools of his time and converted in 1875 and ordained in September, 1884. He was the father of Rev. Leonard Hathaway who also served in Maine. He married Vivania R. Batchelder Hathaway (1846 - 1933) on January 5, 1869.

Rev Wilson Warren Hayden
Birth:
Apr. 28, 1856
Maine
Death:
Jan. 7, 1932
Burial:
South Dover Cemetery
Dover-Foxcroft
Piscataquis County, Maine
Plot: South Section, Row

Leonard Hathaway
Birth:
1802
Middleborough, Mass.,
Death:
Nov. 7, 1876
Burial:
Hathaway Cemetery
Garland, Penobscot County, Maine

A preacher in the F.W.Baptist Denomination fifty-one years. Ordained in 1826. His labors have been in Maine. Died at age 74 yrs.29 ds.

*Inscription:
Front *I have finished the work which thou gavest me to do.*
Back:*The gospel which he preached for more than fifty years sustained him to the last.*
Right:*Faithfully he done the work of the ministry Firmly he kept the faith Surely he wears the crown. Sacred is his memory.*

"Hayden, Rev. Wilson Warren, son of H. W. and Cynthia A. (Bigelow) Hayden, was born in Corinna, Me. He was converted when eleven years of age. He prepared for college in the Corinna Union Academy and the Maine Central Institute, finishing in 1876. He graduated from Bates College, Lewiston, in 1881, and from Bates Theological School in 1884. June 7, 1882, he received license to preach from the Exeter Q. M., and Aug. 14, 1884, was ordained by the Lisbon Q. M., N. H., and became pastor of the Whitefield church. June 17, 1884, he married Miss Cora R. Lambert.

Benjamin Francis Hayes
Birth:
Mar. 28, 1830
New Gloucester
Cumberland County, Maine
Death:
Feb. 27, 1906
Lewiston
Androscoggin County, Maine
Burial:
Riverside Cemetery
Lewiston
Androscoggin County, Maine
Plot: 0304

Rev. Benjamin Francis Hayes, D.D. son of Rev. Jesse and Mary (Harmon) Hayes. He fitted for college at the Lewiston Falls Academy (Edward Little Institute), Auburn, ME. He graduated from Bowdoin College in 1855, and from the Theological Seminary at New Hampton, N.H. in 1858. He was a teacher of sciences and German in New Hampton Literary Institution 1855-59. Converted in 1843, he was baptized in August. He was ordained in 1859 by the Rhode Island Association and May 1st entered upon a pastorate at Olneyville, R.I.

August, 1863, he became principal of Lapham Institute, which office he filled till July 1865. Since that date he has been professor in Bates College (professor of modern languages 1865-69, of intellectual and moral philosophy since 1869); and since 1873 he has been also professor of exegetical theology in the theological department of the college.

He studied at Halle, Germany, with Ulrici, 1873-74. He was appointed acting president of the college 1877-78, during the absence of the president in Europe. He has been connected with our schools or colleges as teacher or superintendent ever since his graduation in 1855.

He has been vice-president and acting president of the Foreign Mission Society, member of the Home Mission, Education, and (since 1873) the Printing Establishment boards. In 1862 he was a delegate to General Conference, and in 1880 preached the centennial sermon at Weir's. He married Aug. 12, 1856, Miss Arcy Carry, dau. Of Francis and Sally Cary, of Turner, ME. (From ME Birth records).Of Prof. Hayes' three children, Rev. Francis L. Hayes is pastor at Boston, and Elizabeth is wife of Rev. A. E. Cox." Another son, is Elwood Cary Hayes, b. 1868, m. Annie Lee Bean, 21 Oct. 1895.

Rev Jesse Hayes
Birth:
1797
Death:
1865
Burial:
Riverside Cemetery
Lewiston
Androscoggin County
Maine

Father of Benjamin Francis Hayes who was a noted theologian and once president of Bates College.

Joseph Higgins
Birth:
1776
Death:
1837

Burial:
Thorndike Center Cemetery
Thorndike, Waldo County, Maine

Rev. Joseph Higgins of Thorndike, Maine, aged 91 years, and his wife, Betsey Higgins, aged 89 years, both died on the 5th of February, 1867, and within ten hours of each other, by no especial sickness except the gradual breaking down of old age. Father Higgins was born in Eastham, Mass., in 1776. Mother Higgins, whose maiden name was Files, was born in Gorham, Maine, in 1778. He came to Thorndike, then called Lincoln Plantation, and felled the first tree on the farm where he ever afterwards lived, in 1797, being one of the very first settlers in town. They were married in 1804, were blessed with eight children, all of whom lived to have families of their own. One of the two sons, Joseph Higgins, Esq., has always lived on the farm with his father and had three children. Still there had never been a death on that dear old homestead until father and mother Higgins passed over the Jordan together. He retained his mental faculties and physical strength in an unusual manner - enjoying life, and contributing to the enjoyment of others till the last days of his life. She was a devoted and cheerful Christian and a most affectionate wife and mother, and although her memory failed, and she was quite childish for the last few years, yet her happy disposition and social, buoyant spirit continued with her to the end. Father Higgins had a good education for his time and taught the first three schools ever taught in Thorndike.

He experienced religion in 1803 and joined the Freewill Baptist Church organized there in that year. He commenced preaching in 1806 and was ordained in 1811. He was an honor to his profession to the day of his death. He worked on his farm through the week and preached on the Sabbathentirely without salary, as was the custom in those days. His preaching was candid, Practical, and very scriptural, the Bible being his chief book of study. The Freewill Baptist Church in Thorndike owes much of its strength and prosperity to father Higgins. For years he preached and lived when many ministers would have been discouraged. And for many years last past, having voluntarily resigned the pastorate, his life, advice, sympathy and means have been a great help to those who have ministered to that church and people. He was a most conscientious and exemplary man in his daily life, showing love to God, man and his country. He was prompt and accurate in his business affairs and quite successful in temporal as well as spiritual things. They gave their eight children a good home and school education, so that they are among the most respectable and influential members of society. Seven of them are living, and they were all present at the funeral, and the aged parents lived to see all their children worthy members of Christian churches. Their life work so perfectly done, there is a pleasing sublimity in the fact that these venerable parents were taken together from earth to heaven. And it adds to the moral grandeur of the scene when we remember that it can literally and truthfully be said of them in the language of scripture, "And they were both righteous before God, walking in all the commandments and ordinances of the Lord blameless." (Written by E. Knowlton in the "Morning Star"

Albert G. Hill
Birth:
Apr. 27, 1838
Newfield
York County, Maine
Death:
Jan. 26, 1907
Garland
Penobscot County, Maine
Burial:
Mount Pleasant Cemetery
Dexter
Penobscot County, Maine
He attended the Parsonfield Seminary and New Hampton Institution. In 1858 he was converted and was licensed in 1867 and ordained by the Cumberland Quarterly Meeting in 1869.

Rev James W. Hinckley
Birth:
Mar. 12, 1827
Industry
Franklin County
Maine
Death:
Aug. 22, 1908
Burial:
Mount Rest Cemetery
Athens
Somerset County
Maine

"Rev. James W. Hinckley, son of Josiah and Mercy (Williams) Hinckley. He was converted on this thirtieth birthday, and Jan. 3, 1862, received license. He was ordained Dec. 25, 1863, and has been pastor of the Brighton, Athens, Harmony, Cambridge, and Parkman churches, where in eight years he baptized thirty converts. He now (1887) resided at Athens and supplies as occasion requires. On Jan. 23, 1850, he married Miss Mary J. Ladd.

Elder Henry Hobbs, Sr
Birth:
Mar. 3, 1768
Berwick
York County
Maine
Death: Mar. 20, 1848
Waterboro
York County
Maine
Burial:
Hobbs/Knights Cemetery
Waterboro
York County
Maine

Rev. Henry Hobbs, Sr., began to preach in 1798, and strengthened the church in Waterborough, which had recently been reorganized with eight members by P(elatiah) Tingley. The rest of the church had gone with their pastor to the Baptists.
In January, 1800, he visited the Farmington Q.M. with John Buzzell, and assisted in quieting the Locke trouble. He was ordained in Standish, May 22, 1801.
He was one of the original peitioners in 1804 to the Legislature of Massachusetts for a recognition and incorporation of the "Freewill Anti-pedo Baptists" of Maine. It was his sonorous voice

which was heard over a mile distant during the grove reformation in August 1808, and which brought Rev. Henry Leach to a sense of his sin. He was clerk of the Parsonfield Q.M.(Quarterly Meeting), and treasurer of the "Maine Freewill Baptist Charitable Society" from its organization, Nov. 27, 1824.

In 1825 he was one of the nine who assumed financial responsibility for the publication of the first *"Morning Star."* In February, 1826, he was chairman of the meeting at which the legal company was organized for the publication of the paper. The printing house was known as Hobbs, Woodman & Co. From this press John Buzzell issued his "Life of Benjamin Randall," in 1827.

H. Hobbs was six years a proprietor of the *"Morning Star,"* and in 1832 was on the publishing committee for a year. He was one of the committee of twelve to whom the call for a General Conference of the denomination was referred by the Y.M.(Yearly Meeting) at Parsonfield in November, 1826. He was a member of the Second General Conference in 1828, and chairman of the business and standing committees. He was moderator of the third General Conference and preached the opening sermon. He also sat in the fifth and sixth sessions of the General Conference.

He represented the district of Maine in the Massachusetts Legislature, and was a member of the convention which drafted the constitution of Maine. He

subsequently served in the Legislature, and was on the Governor's council several times. He was a man of strong mind and good business tact. He was an exellent presiding officer. Rev. O.H. Tracy is a great-grandson."

Andrew Hobson
Birth:
Sep. 10, 1795
Buxton,
York County, Maine
Death:
May 1, 1877
Cambridge,
Middlesex County,
Massachusetts
Burial:
Steep Falls Cemetery,
Steep Falls,
Cumberland County, Maine

He was converted at age 21, under the labors of Rev. Clement Phinney, was baptized by Rev. Jonathan Clay, and united with the Free Baptist church in Buxton. He began to preach in 1821, and was ordained two years after. He pastored several churches, including So. Gorham, Buxton, fifteen yrs and built a new meeting house there, Fort Hill, Steep Falls, ten yrs. He returned to Steep Falls in 1862, and in ten years baptized over fifty. In 1871, he entered upon his last pastorate which was at Hollis. He was one of a committee of twelve in favor of establishing a General Conference, and was a member of the first and of several other General Conferences. He was one of the original trustees of the "Morning Star" (newspaper). Every genuine interest received his sympathy. He had one son, Pelatiah M. who became a Free Will Baptist minister.

He was educated at Parsonfield Seminary (later Bates) and Gorham Academy, and was a member of the first class in the Biblical School at Parsonsfield. He received license from the Gorham Quarterly Meeting in 1842, and was ordained by the Bowdoin QM, at Bath, ME, in July, 1843. He was pastor of the North Street church, Bath, and remained two years, baptizing about twenty. He engaged in business with his father at Steep Falls. He helped build up the church there, which was organized in 1847. Beginning in the spring of 1856, he was pastor of this church three years, and added sixty to its membership, forty by baptism.

Pelatiah M. Hobson
Birth:
Jul. 20, 1818
West Buxton,
York County, Maine
Death:
Jan. 8, 1888
Steep Falls,
Cumberland County, Maine
Burial:
Steep Falls Cemetery,
Steep Falls,
Cumberland County, Maine

Alphonso L Houghton
Birth:
May 3, 1847
Weld, Me
Death:
Oct. 2, 1881
Weld, Me
Burial:
Oak Grove Cemetery
Bath, Sagadahoc County, Maine

He was the eldest child of Azel E. and Betsey (Hawes) Houghton. "When about sixteen years of age he became a Christian, was baptized by Rev. Orin Pitts and united with the church. He graduated from Bates College in 1870, as valedictorian of his class, and at once entered the Theological School. During this course he was a tutor in the college. In May, 1872, he received a unanimous call to the church in Lawrence, Mass. He accepted the call and began his labors there in July ; was ordained and installed Sept. 4. Jan. I, 1873, he married Miss Hattie B. Mallet, of Bath, Me., in whose death, three years later, he was grievously afflicted. He held the pastorate eight years, when broken health compelled him to resign. As a minister, the scholar and pastor were most finely blended. He was an organizer. Besides the addition of nearly three hundred members to the church during his pastorate, he trained the church into such order and efficiency that, when he was cut off, the church went on steadily with its work. For several years he served on the school committee in Lawrence. He was a member of the executive board of the Foreign Mission Society, and a trustee of Bates College. He left his excellent library and $1,000 to this institution, $500 to the permanent fund of the Bible School in India, and a microscope and cabinet of minerals to Maine Central Institute. After seeking recovery in Europe and in Colorado, he returned to his native place shortly before his death.

Francis Howard
Birth:
Nov. 2, 1810
Ward, Maine
Death:
Feb. 11, 1892
Washington
Knox County, spaceMaine
Burial:
Howard Cemetery
Knox County, Maine

His conversion happened when he was 13 years of age. In 1843 he was licensed and the same year ordained. He labored in many revivals and was a pastor eight years. He has baptized 74 and attended 412 funerals.

Rev. Richard L. HOWARD
Birth:
Mar. 24, 1824
Oxford
Chenango County
New York
Death:
Dec. 11, 1902
Limerick
York County
Maine
Burial:
Highland Cemetery
Limerick
York County
Maine
Plot: Tier 10--3

"Rev. Richard L. HOWARD was the brother of Rev. Geo.H. Howard, His parents were Anson M. and Bershabee L. (Lawrence) HOWARD. His father was clerk of the Susquehanna Y.M.., and of the Owego Q.M. He was baptized by Rev. Asa Dodge, at the age of ten, and reclaimed when thirty-two years of age, beginning to preach the next year. He received an academic education in the town of Union, N.Y. In June 1857, he was licensed, and in December was ordained by the Boone Co. Q.M., Ill., to preach for the Freewill Baptists. He organized two churches in Moniteau Co. Missouri, and baptized thirty or more, among whom was his brother, Rev. G.H. Howard.

He labored with the churches in the Quincy Q.M., Ill, and was pastor of all its churches, organizing two and baptizing over two hundred.

He enlisted in the summer of 1862, as first Lieutenant in the 124th Ill. Infantry, and had command of his company through the Vicksburg campaign under Grant; was promoted to the chaplaincy in Sept. 1863, and served till the close of the war.

In 1865 he became pastor of the Commerce church, Mich. In 1870 he took chqarge of the "*Christian Freeman,*" Chicago, and after a year settled with the Mt. Pleasant church at Racine, Wis. He was called to Fairport, N.Y., in 1873; to the Pine St. church, Lewiston, ME, in 1876; to Bangor in 1879, and in March 1885, he entered pastorate at Franconia, N.H. In these churches he has baptized over five hundred. He raised the debt of the Bangor church, of $3,000, in his last winter there. He is a member of the executive committee of the Home Mission Society, and has been a member of General Conferences in 1868, 1874, 1880 and 1886. He was trustee of Hillsdale College ten years, of Maine Central Institute six years, a trustee of the New Hampton

Institution, N.H. While in Maine he was president of the Maine State Sunday-School Association two years, and chaplain of the Grand Army in Maine eight years.

He has published a history of his regiment. He was on the school board of Bangor five years, the last three chairman, and done similar service at Franconia. Sept. 3, 1853, he married Miss Clara J. Nelson, it being his second marriage, and had three children. Among whom was the Rev. George N. Howard."

Rev James A Howe
Birth:
Oct. 10, 1834
Massachusetts
Death:
Dec. 29, 1918
Lewiston
Androscoggin County, Maine
Burial:
Riverside Cemetery
Lewiston
Androscoggin County, Maine
Plot: 0643

Rev. James A. Howe, D.D., (Hillsdale College, 1876) brother of Rev. Geo. W. Howe, was raised near Centralville, by pious parents, serving in the Lowell church for over forty-two years as most useful members. Their home was known for its Christian hospitality. James A. was converted under the labors of Rev. O.T. Moulton, and soon after united with the church. He studied a term at Smithville Seminary and another at North Hampton, NH. He prepared for college with his elder brother under the able teacher, and in 1856 entered the sophomore class of Bowdoin College, graduating in 1859.He studied in the Biblical School at New Hampton, and at Andover Seminary, and accepted the church at Blackstone, Mass., where he was ordained by the Rhode Island Association. The next year he married Miss Rachel E. Rogers of Upper Stillwater, ME.After a pastorate of eighteen months he was pastor for over eight years at Olneyville, R.I. Here he added 104 to the church, sixty-two of them by baptism. He resigned in 1872, to accept a chair of theology in the theological department of Bates College.

John Hull
Birth:
unknown
Death:
Aug. 19, 1829
Livermore
Androscoggin County, Maine
Burial:
Turner Village Cemetery
Turner
Androscoggin County, Maine

In Freewill Baptist records as a minister. Aged 31.He was of Nova Scotia.

Eld Samuel Hutchins
Birth:
Nov. 29, 1790
New Portland, Me.
Death:
Apr. 9, 1876
West Waterville, Me.
Burial:
East New Portland Cemetery
New Portland, Somerset County,
Maine

He was converted when twelve years of age, and began to preach at the age of nineteen. In 1810, at the age of twenty, he was ordained and became the first settled minister in New Portland. Previous to his marriage, he taught school and preached in Madison. He witnessed several revivals there. In Mt. Vernon many were converted under his labors. He also preached in Boston, Mass., Portland, Bangor, and Augusta. He was pastor at Norridgewock several years. He then moved to Belgrade, and was pastor of the church there and at the same time at Smithfield, till his death. He baptized more than 1,000 persons, and his labors "were widely known and appreciated throughout the Kennebec Y. M. For several years he was military chaplain. He was a representative in the Legislature two or three years, and while there preached in Portland. He was a member of the Second and Third General Conferences. Inscription: Age 85y 4m 10d.

Leonard Hutchins

Birth:
April 20, 1828
New Portland, Maine
Death:
1915
Burial:
East New Portland Cemetery
New Portland
Somerset County, Maine

His mother died when he was 12 years old and three years later he was converted. He studied in the schools near him, and dwelt with his father until the father's death in May, 1868. He had been licensed in June, 1853 and was ordained September 21, 1856. He entered Bangor Theological Seminary in 1869. He pastored a number of churches in the area and had revival interest in each of his churches, baptizing 50 in Garland, and about 150 and other pastorates. From 1883 through 1887 he was employed in missionary work by the Maine State Mission Society in Anson Quarterly Meeting having under his care the churches in Stark, Freeman and Salem, Lexington and Dead River. He was the clerk and treasurer of the Anson Quarterly Meeting and also was a trustee of the Maine Central Institute.

Asa Foster Hutchinson

Birth:
Aug. 1, 1824
Buckfield, Maine
Death:
Dec. 2, 1893
South Portland, Maine

Burial:
Mountain View Cemetery
Auburn
Androscoggin County, Maine

His parents were Rev. Samuel and Mercy (Randall) Hutchison, and a cousin to Rev. C. T. Keen. He was converted at 15 and studied in North Bridgeton Academy, Maine and in Strafford Academy and in the Biblical School at Whitestown, New York. He was licensed in September, 1845 and ordained in September, 1850. He pastored many churches in that area and baptized 185 converts. He was on school committees in various towns and in 1865 he represented the towns of West Garndiner, Farmingdale, and Pittston in the legislature.

Rev Ebenezer Hutchinson

Birth:
Mar., 1818
Scarborough
Cumberland County, Maine
Death:
Sep. 29, 1865
Maine
Burial:
Bay View Cemetery
South Portland Gardens
Cumberland County, Maine

Rev. Ebenezer Hutchinson, bro. of Rev. Asa F. Hutchinson, was born in Scarborough, ME..

At age nineteen he united with the Baptist church in Dover ME. He entered the Parsonfield Seminary under Hosea Quinby soon after where he joined the the Free Baptists. He was licensed by the Otisfield Quarterly Meeting and saw many converted in an itinerant ministry.

In 1843 he married Miss Frances Dyer, of Cape Elizabeth, and for several years gave his attention to teaching. In 1856 he was ordained as pastor of the Cape Elizabeth church and in five years which followed many were converted, and the meeting-house enlarged and improved. He now completed a course of medicine which he had left unfinished years before, and prosecutd successfully that practice, preaching only occasionally.

He enlisted early in the Civil War in the Twenty-fifth Maine Regiment, and served nine months He contracted consumption, from which he died in camp in 1863,

---

Elder Joseph Hutchinson
Birth:
1755
Penobscot County
Maine
Death:
Feb. 24, 1801
Hebron
Oxford County, Maine
Burial:
Bog Brook Cemetery
Hebron

Oxford County
Maine

Rev. Joseph Hutchinson moved with his father to Windham about 1780.

He married Rebecca, daughter of Joseph and Ann Legro, of Marblehead, Mass, in 1778, and had eleven children.

He was the first minister of the denomination to die. As early as 1790, he was ruling elder and an unordained preacher, and nine years later he was ordained. He was present at the Y.M. at Anson, ME, in 1800, and chairman of an important committee. At the beginning of the year 1801, he visited with a friend the members of the church, and seemed impressed with the necessity of diligence. He would call upon a family, speak to them of Christ, kneel and pray, and hasten to the next house. The church was revived, but in the midst of the interest he was taken sick, and on the 24th of February, 1801, in the vigor of manhood, at the age of 40, he passed away.

His funeral was attended by Elder Stinchfield. During twenty years of the denomination, they had increased to thirty in the ministry without a death.

> **NOTE:**
> **He was the first minister to die in the Free Will Baptist denomination.**

Rev Joseph Hutchinson
Birth:
Apr. 11, 1811
Gorham
Cumberland County
Maine
Death:
Jan. 25, 1889
Maine
Burial:
Lane Cemetery
Freeport
Cumberland County, Maine

Rev. Joseph Hutchinson, of East Otisfield, ME, was born in Gorham, ME, April 5, 1811. He was an older brother of Rev's Asa F. and Ebenezer Hutchinson: [all sons of Rev. Samuel and Mercy (Randall) Hutchinson.]

He preached his first sermon on Bailey Hill, Poland, April 1, 1856, and was ordained July 8, 1858. His pastorates have been in Poland, Danville, Sumner, Buckfield, N. Freport, Otisfield, Bridgewater, and Miinot. He has had revivals at each place, and baptized 125 converts and organized two churches.

After three years of suffering he passed to his reward. He married Miss Martha J. Tobey, and has five children living. Two sons served honorably for three years in the war.

Benjamin Jaques
Birth:
1790
Death:
Jul. 16, 1878
Lisbon, Me
Burial:
Riverview Cemetery
Topsham, Sagadahoc County

Jaques died at aged 87 years and 8 months. He was converted in April, 1825, and baptized the next year. He was in the ministry more than forty years.

John B Jordan
Birth:
September 30, 1850
Auburn, Maine
Death:
1925
Burial:
Oak Hill Cemetery
Auburn
Androscoggin County, Maine

He was converted as a boy, and at the age of 16 was baptized. He united with the Court Street church, Auburn. His early education was with a business life and view. In March, 1868, when 17 years of age he accepted the position of messenger and bookkeeper in the First National Bank of Auburn, and was promoted in 1871 to the position of Teller, and in February, 1874, was elected cashier, which office he held until 1882, when he resigned and accepted a call to the pastorate of the Pine Street church, Lewiston, Maine. For a number of years he was active in evangelistic work in connection with the YMCA. He received license to preach June 11, 1878 and was ordained on may 25, 1882. During his pastorate with the Pine Street church 122 were added to its membership, 100 by baptism. In August 1883, he accepted a call to the first church, in Minneapolis, Minnesota. He remained with this church until October,, 1885 but not before 53 had been added to the church. There after he became pastor of the Augusta church in July, 1886. During the first year, 30 were added to the church. In December, 1886 he was elected chaplain of the Maine Insane Hospital. He was a member of the General Conference in 1886. He was the corresponding Sec. of the Maine Home Missionary Society and clerk of the Maine Central Yearly Meeting. He was a member of the city Council of Auburn for two.

Rev Columbus T Keene
Birth:
Feb. 21, 1832
Death:
Jul. 22, 1901
Burial:
Buckfield Village Cemetery
Buckfield
Oxford County
Maine

Rev. Columbus T. Keen, son of Nathaniel and Lydia (Hutchinson) Keen, was converted in the winter of 1857-58. Licensed in November 1881, he was ordained by the Otisfield Q.M. in September, 1884. He has held pastorates at West Mt. Vernon, Wells Mills, East Buckfield, and from 1886 at E. Hebron, a church reorganized in 1838 from the old First church founded by the grandfather of Mr. Keen, the Rev. Joseph Hutchinson. He has labored a number of years in the Y.M.C.A., and in 1884 was engaged as Minnesota state missionary for six months. He married Martha M. Boody, Nov. 16, 1855, and has five children.

William P. Kinney
Birth:
Mar. 7, 1833
Queensberry
New Brunswick, Canada
Death:
1916
Maine
Burial:
Old Baptist Cemetery
Yarmouth
Cumberland County, Maine

He became a Christian at the age of 16 and was educated in the Houlton Academy and Bangor Theological Seminary. His license to preach was granted on March 15, 1873, and on March 17, 1881 he was ordained. He held eight pastorates and several revivals and baptized 20 convert. He helped organize four churches. He was clerk of the quarterly meeting for a number of years and was a trustee of the Maine Central Institute and a member of the legislature of 1876.

Rev Charles L Kirkland
Birth:
1843
New Brunswick, Canada
Death:
Apr. 15, 1912

Burial:
Mattawamkeag Cemetery
Mattawamkeag
Penobscot County
Maine,

Note: "Buried at Sea" He was lost on the "Titanic"

Elder Ebenezer Knowlton, Sr
Birth:
unknown
Death:
Nov. 18, 1841
Burial:
Pine Grove Cemetery
South Montville
Waldo County, Maine

He was a Freewill Baptist minister, per town records: Descendants of Jonathan Towle : "They lived in Chichester and had twelve children." *Town Records - Vol.2 - p.68: "Pittsfield, March 22, 1808. This may certify the Selectmen of Chichester and all others whomsoever it may concern;

that Mr. Joshua Towle of Chichester doth belong to the freewill-Baptist Society and doth attend meeting with us when it convenient - given under my hand. El. Ebenezer Knowlton of Pittsfield"

He was married to Abigail True Knowlton (____ - 1868)

Ebenezer Knowlton
Birth:
Dec. 6, 1815
Pittsfield, N. H.
Death:
Sep. 10, 1874
Montville, Me.
Burial:
Pine Grove Cemetery
South Montville, Waldo County, Maine

His father moved to Montville in 1828. He obtained a thorough academic education and became a teacher in early life. He was converted in 1832, and united with the church in Montville. The day that he decided to preach the gospel was the day he was elected speaker in the Legislature of his state. He preached his first sermon at Hallowell, Aug. 9, 1846, from the words" We love him because he first loved us." He was ordained Dec. 17, 1848. His labors covered a wide territory in eastern and central Maine. He preached in Rockland two years at different times. The rest of his ministry was in connection with the Montville churches. He went far and near to solemnize marriages, attend funerals and deliver temperance and Sunday-school addresses. At the close of 1852, he wrote in his journal: "number' of funerals attended during the year, sixty; sermons preached, 171; religious meetings attended, 332; temperance and Sunday school lectures, twenty-three." In 1853 the Legislature elected him State Treasurer, but he declined the honor.

He consented, however, in 1854, to be elected to Congress, upon the advice of his brethren, but declined a re-electiion in order to devote himself to the work of the ministry and also to work for the Maine State Seminary. When he accepted the nomination to Congress he informed the convention that nominated him, that if elected, he should go to Congress as a Christian minister devoted to the interests of humanity; that he would accept the nomination only as from freemen desiring to be represented by a freeman; that he should allow no allegiance to any clique or party in any way to interfere with a strict adherence to freedom, country, and God. While in Congress he wrote weekly letters to the *Morning Star,* subscribing himself "Daniel" This correspondence attracted considerable attention. He took an interest in the colored people and preached the gospel to them. He preached one half of the Sabbaths during the time he was in Congress. In 1869, there was a general desire among the Republicans of Maine that he should be their candidate for Governor. But although great pressure was brought to bear upon him and he was himself disposed to consent for the sake of the principles of temperance, he finally refused to allow his name to be used. Mr. Knowlton had all the mental and moral qualities that go to make up the real statesman, such as ability, strength, foresight, decision, honesty, integrity, love of humanity, and fear of God; and the only reason he did not rise to higher positions in the affairs of state was because he declined to do so, believing that, as a minister of Christ, he was holding the highest office on earth. When urged to become a candidate for Governor, he wrote to a leading religious politician saying, among other things: "You urge me to be Governor so as to enforce prohibition. I know rum-selling is a crime and grog-shops are a nuisance. A radical law with front teeth and grinders should be kept on the statute book and be lived up to.

But a correct moral sentiment among the people is the only means to secure this end. This moral sentiment grows only out of the gospel. The Christian ministry is the leading agency in spreading the gospel. So do let me alone, that what there is left of me may be devoted to the appropriate work of my profession. It is easier to find good and suitable material to make governors of, than it is to find good and suitable material to make ministers. It is but little I can do anywhere, but I would rather see one young man in my congregation soundly converted to Christ than to have any office in the gift of man." He was often appointed to preach at denominational gatherings, but accepted with extreme diffidence. He was desired as pastor in Lewiston, Auburn, Augusta, Portland, Boston, New York and other places, but accepted none of these positions. He was very firm in his denominational loyalty.

He was one of the projectors of the Maine State Seminary, which grew into Bates College.

Other positions of responsibility were as follows: Trustee of Colby University, trustee of Bates College, president of the Foreign Mission Society, corporator of the Printing Establishment, and moderator of three General Conferences. He died suddenly while taking a bath in a pond near his home, where he was accustomed to fish and swim. His death was conspicuously noticed by resolutions in town meeting, and by the denomination in which he was a pillar of strength.

Zina Knowlton
Birth:
Sep. 20, 1813
Swanville
Waldo County, Maine
Death:
Sep. 7, 1885
Monroe
Waldo County, Maine
Burial:
Mount Solitude Cemetery
Monroe
Waldo County, Maine

Married Nov 2 1833 in Swanville and was a Free Will Baptist minister.

Elliot Sawyer Lamb
Birth:
May 26, 1810
Vermont
Death:
Jun. 17, 1888
Weld
Franklin County, Maine
Burial:
West Leeds Cemetery
Leeds
Androscoggin County, Maine,

Elliot was the son of Luther and Lucretia (Lamb) Lamb. He had at least three siblings. Though his death record and census records say he was born in Vermont, his biographical sketch in the "Free Baptist Cyclopedia" says he was born in Canaan, New Hampshire, but his family moved to Vershire, Vermont shortly after his birth. When Elliot was 17, his family moved to Leeds. He was converted at the age of 20 and baptized by Rev. Silas Curtis.

On May 27, 1832 he married Julia A. Stanley. Julia had been a founding member of the Free Will Baptist Church in North Leeds, when established in 1829.

Elliot and Julia lived in West Leeds on River Road, in a house almost immediately across the road from the entrance to this cemetery. They had two children: Orissa and a son born in 1848. Vital records say his name was William Elliot, however the census records say his name was Hurbert (or similar name spelling). This son likely died young, as the Cyclopaedia said Orissa was Elliot's only child.

Elliot was ordained in 1842. The 1850 census said he was a minister for the Free Will Baptist Church, though the 1860 census said he was a house carpenter. According to the Cyclopedia he preached most of the time, and participated in revivals in numerous Maine towns.

After Julia died Elliot moved to Weld to help his brother care for their father. There Elliot remarried to Rozillah Lawrence on May 15, 1874. They lived on the farm her father had owned in Weld. He organized a church in Weld, and baptized 40 converts.

George Lamb
Birth:
1788
Lincolnville,
Waldo County, Maine
Death:
Dec. 14, 1836
Brunswick,
Cumberland County, Maine
Burial:
Growstown Cemetery,
Brunswick,
Cumberland County, Maine

He became interested in religion when but a boy, and was converted and joined the Free Will Baptist Church. His circumstances afforded him little advantage of an education, but he had an inquisitive and well-balanced mind, he worked with a clergyman in his preaching endeavors, and his success was such that he was licensed and ordained in 1813. He gathered a church in Bangor Me, but he declined settlement. His brethren wanted him to go to Topsham where the church was waning. There was a remarkable revival commenced and he baptized about 40. (It was here that the later eminent scholar, Prof. John J. Butler, was influenced by good from Rev. George Lamb, with whom he stayed while a student there.

John Lamb
Birth:
Jun. 7, 1776
Nova Scotia, Canada
Death:
Jun. 4, 1828
Waldo County, Maine
Burial:
Center Lincolnville Burying Ground
Waldo County, Maine

In 1805 he was ordained and for 20 years he had a useful ministry. He preached the gospel without any salary and at the same time supported with hard labor a large family. For some time his public ministry was hindered by asthma.

Zachariah Leach
Birth:
Jun. 7, 1765
Raymond
Cumberland County, Maine
Death:
Nov. 3, 1841
Raymond
Cumberland County, Maine
Burial:
Raymond Village Cemetery
Raymond
Cumberland County, Maine

He was ordained a Free Will Baptist minister on Nov. 6, 1794 by Rev. Benjamin Randall, and others. In 1799 he became clerk of the Edgecomb Q. M. In 1808 he had an extensive reformation at Standish, in which Joseph White was

converted and soon became an efficient minister. He preached three times at the Y. M. at Edgecomb in September 1811. He was followed by John Buzzell and John Colby. March 18,1812, he wrote to the *Religous Magazine* of an agreeable journey he had among the churches of the Sandy River country. He made the ordaining prayer while Joseph White preached the sermon at the ordination of Clement Phinney at Standish Neck in 1816. In 1834 he added forty-six to his church by baptism and the next year twenty-nine.

Rev Daniel Blaisdell Lewis
Birth:
Mar. 1, 1804
Cornish
York County
Maine
Death:
Oct. 16, 1859
Waterville
Kennebec County

Maine
Burial:
Pine Grove Cemetery
Waterville
Kennebec County
Maine

His parents moved with him to Waterville, where, at the age of twenty, he publicly convessed Christ, and the next year was baptized by Rev. L. Lewis. He soon saw his duty clearly, and after deep conviction, began to preach. He was licensed, and in 1831 was ordained by the Exeter Quarterly Meeting in Pittsfield, ME.

For thirty years the Sabbath nearly always found him at his post preaching Jesus. His evenings he gave to study and to preparation for his ministry. In Sydney, Waterville, Smithfield, Belgrade, Mt. Vernon, Readfield, Unity and Thorndike he went organizing churches and baptizing converts. He has been called "quite the father of the Waterville Q.M." He was a modest, unassuming preacher, firm and unwavering in his faith, earnest and effective in his appeals.

Samuel Lewis
Birth:
1825
Buxton, Maine
Death:
Oct. 12, 1850
Burial:
Hackett-Notch Cemetery
New Vineyard
Franklin County, Maine

At the age of 24 he married Phepe Irish. He was converted at the age of 28 and was baptized by John Buzzell. He moved to Chatham, New Hampshire and began to preach and some years later he moved to Harrison, Maine where he had great revivals. He was ordained in Sebec Quarterly Meeting in 1832 and was instrumental in promoting revivals in this new section and organizing and sustaining several of the hurches that composed Springfield Quarterly Meeting.

Rev Stephen Lewis
Birth:
Jan. 5, 1781
Boothbay
Lincoln County
Maine
Death:
Mar. 14, 1856
Burial:
Highland Cemetery
Jefferson
Lincoln County, Maine

Rev. Stephen Lewis, died at his residence in Augusta, ME, aged 77[sic] years. He was licensed to preach April 17, 1830, by the Edgecomb Quarterly Meeting and ordained in Whitefield Nov. 7, 1834. He spent most of his ministerial labors in Windsor, and in the Edgecomb Q.M.

He was devoted to the spiritual welfare of his people and deeply intrested in all the benevolent enterprises of the day.

Almon Libby
Birth:
Oct. 10, 1816
Minot, Maine
Death:
Nov. 1, 1895
Burial:
Stroudwater Burying Ground
Portland
Cumberland County, Maine

He became a Christian at the age of 16 and was a student in the Parsonfield Seminary. In 1837 he was ordained by the Cumberland Quarterly Meeting. All of his pastorates were in the state of Maine. He labored in many revivals and baptized a large number of converts. In 1886 he was an agent for the Androscroggin County Bible Society. He has been a member of the General Conference. He had two sons that graduated from Bates College; one is a civil engineer, and the other is a district attorney in Colorado. His youngest daughter was on the staff of the Lewiston Journal.

David Libby
Birth:
Jun. 2, 1822 Portland,
Cumberland County,
Maine
Death:
1901
Burial:
Lisbon Cemetery, Lisbon,
Androscoggin County, Maine

He was a younger brother of Rev. Almon Libby. He became a Christian when fourteen years of age; was licensed in June 1845, and ordained by the Bowdoin Quarterly Meeting, two years later. He had pastorates in South Lewiston, Harrison, Harpswell, Freeport, Poland and Lisbon. He baptized a large number of converts.

James Libby
Birth:
Oct., 1796
Auburn,
Androscoggin County, Maine
Death:
Mar. 6, 1884
West Poland,
Androscoggin County, Maine
Burial:
Highland Cemetery,
West Poland,
Androscoggin County, Maine

Rev. James Libby, became a Christian at the age of twenty, was baptized by Elder Leach and joined the church in that vicinity. In 1828, after serious conviction, he consecrated himself to the ministry, and was ordained at Danville by Rev's Z. Jordan, J. White and J. Clay. In 1832, he moved to West Poland, and for thirty-three years was pastor of that church. Early in his pastorate a meeting house was erected. There were several extensive revivals with large additions to the church. The Second Poland church grew out of this church. In the course of his ministry of more than sixty years, he baptized about one thousand converts, married several hundred couples and attended the funerals of 1500 persons. His valuable labors were frequently sought by various pastors in protracted meeting.

What A Day That Will Be When My Saviour I Shall See!

Elder Ward Locke
Birth
1784
Death:
Nov. 25, 1828
Chesterville, Maine
Burial:
Chesterville Center Cemetery
Chesterville
Franklin County, Maine

He began to preach in 1806 and was ordained in 1818. His ministry was in Maine. He was a delegate to the General Conference in 1827.

Jason Mariner
Birth:
November 14, 1824
Lincolnville, Maine
Death:
Nov. 18, 1891
Burial:
Union Cemetery
Lincolnville Center
Waldo County, Maine

He was converted through the Ministry of Rev. John Stevens who baptized him at the age of 18 when he fully gave his heart to God. He preached his first sermon on 14, 1843 in the same church where he was converted. He was a student at Whitestown, New York after which he was licensed at Montville Quarterly Meeting and ordained at Lincolnville with Rev. Ebenezer Knowlton preaching. He held numerous pastorates in New York, Maine, Massachusetts, and Rhode Island. He was a trustee of the Maine State Seminary and Bates College for 25 years.

Moses McFarland
Birth:
Unknown
Death:
Nov. 1, 1865
Burial:
Mount Repose Cemetery
Montville
Waldo County, Maine

He was ordained in 1806 and nine in May. In 1818, 40 were converted under his labors and the Second Montville church was organized.

Early in 1827, he was charged with preaching Universalism. Rev. Ebenezer Knowlton of Pittsfield, New Hampshire had moved to the area in time to save the church from defection. At the June Quarterly Meeting a charge was brought against McFarland. In September a committee of seven was appointed, with Rev. Benjamin Thorn as chairman. McFarland finally separated from the quarter meeting in December, 1827.

Elbridge L McKindsley
Birth:
1839
Whitefield, Maine
Death:
1911
Burial:
Whitefield Cemetery
Whitefield
Lincoln County,, Maine

He was converted to the age of 13 and studied at Pittston Academy he was licensed in September 1883 and was ordained in September 1886. He preached as an evangelist most of his ministry.

Death Is The Setting Free From The Warfare Of The Soul

John Miller
Birth:
May 13, 1806
Durham
Androscoggin County, Maine
Death:
Dec. 5, 1869
Durham
Androscoggin County, Maine
Burial:
Union Cemetery
Auburn, Androscoggin County, Maine

Rev George Zeigler Mears
Birth:
Feb. 2, 1799
Bristol,
Maine
Death:
Mar., 1881
Washington
Knox County,
Maine
Burial:
Morrill Village Cemetery
Morrill
Waldo County, Maine

Listed in minister's roll of deceased ministers in 1881, Maine Freewill Bapt. ministers.
1st Wife Abigail Wentworth (mar. Oct. 6, 1821; 2nd wife Elizabeth Rust Neal (ME mar. records) Married: Aug. 18, 1860.

He was converted in 1829 and began to preach with the Methodists in 1837. He afterwards joined the Free Baptists and continued a good and acceptable minister with them until his death. He felt especially called to preach to the poor, and his labors were fruitful. He was a man of much prayer, strong faith, fervent love, and deep piety. He was married to Hannah, dau. of Samuel and Catherine (Clark) Robinson on 2 Dec 1830.

David Moody
Birth:
December 3, 1804
GilmanTon, New Hampshire
Death:
Mar. 7, 1878
Burial:
Mount Solitude Cemetery
Monroe
Waldo County, Maine

Samuel Plummer Morrill
Birth:
February 11, 1816
Chesterville,
Maine
Death:
1892
Burial:
Chesterville Hill Cemetery
Chesterville
Franklin County, Maine

He was converted at age 18, and received his license the following of May, 1824 and was ordained two years later by Rev's. Enoch Place, S. B. Dyer, and Moses Bean, Ebenezer Knowlton and Arthur Caverno. He was in the ministry more than 63 years. The first 10 years was spent in evangelism, with his ministry beginning at Bethlehem, where he had an extensive revival. He helped numerous churches throughout New Hampshire and during this time baptized 171 converts, married 197 couples and attended 572 funerals. On March 19, 1827, he married Miss Sally Bean.

He was a student at the Farmington Academy, and was converted at the age of 18, licensed in 1839 at the age of 23, and ordained in 1841 by the Rev. Dexter Waterman. He held many pastorates in the state of Maine after his ordination, but in 1885 he settled in Vienna, Maine where a good revival was enjoyed. In his 11 pastorates he baptized in all 75. In 1886 he lay aside an active ministry due to poor health. He was a member three times at the Gen. conference; and assisted in organizing several churches. He was elected to the 41st Congress of the United States and served during 1869-70. On November 28, 1838, he married Mary J. Chase.

when a squall hit the boat. The body was found and buried in June on the lake shore. His funeral was attended by Rev. Moses Ames of Garland. He experienced religion about 1834 and was baptized by the Rev. Samuel Lewis, after which he joined the church at Lee. This Sebec Quarterly Meeting granted him a license in January, 1838 and ordained him the following July. He was blessed by revivals in his tours through the Springfield Quarterly Meeting. He had a deep love for the Bible, and was a friend of the Bible school at Whitestown and especially advocated the cause of the slave.

Levi Moulton
Birth:
1812
Death:
May 10, 1846
Burial:
Academy Cemetery
Lee
Penobscot County, Maine

He drowned while crossing a lake in a boat with others coming out of the woods from a lumber drive,

They preached about this time and the hereafter

Rev James Nason
Birth:
Mar. 29, 1829
Lyman
York County,
Maine
Death:
Nov., 1894
Burial:
Oak Grove Cemetery
Wells
York County,
Maine

Rev. James Nason, son of Nehemiah and Olive (Davis) Nason. He received his education in the common schools and in private study. He was converted in March, 1839; licensed by the York County Quarterly Meetinng (QM) in June 1859 and ordained by the Cumberland QM June 7, 1860. He has held pastorates at White Rock, two years; Shapleigh, one year; North Berwick, Beach Ridge, twelve years; Meredith Centre, NH one year; Wells Branch, ME six years; Ross' Corners, two years; Kennebunk, two years; Wells Branch, two years, where he still resides. From four general revivals he has baptized about one hundred. He has assisted in the ordination of four, attended over two hundred funerals and solemnized over one hundred marriages. He was a delegate to the General Conference at Providence, R.I. He married Alice L. Edgecomb, Oct. 8, 1848, and has four sons.

Joseph Nickerson
Birth:
Apr. 10, 1833
Litchfield. Maine
Death:
Feb. 27, 1909
Burial:
Litchfield Plains Cemetery
Litchfield Plains
Kennebec County, Maine

Converted at 17. In December, 1878 he received his licensed to preach and on October 11, 1883 was ordained by Rev. Mark Getchell and others. His pastorates were in the vicinity of his conversion.

Joseph N. Noble
Birth:
Apr. 29, 1847
New Brunswick, Canada
Death:
Feb. 2, 1912
Burial:
Evergreen Cemetery
Houlton
Aroostook County, Maine
Plot: Section 6, Block 13, Grave

He was converted on September 27, 1866 in Canning, Nova Scotia under Rev. Charles Knowles. He yielded the call to preach in May 1882. He was licensed to preach at Upper Woodstock, New Brunswick. In October he began working with the Bridgewater, Maine church, where upon his labors he was ordained by the Houlton Quarterly Meeting on December 18, 1886.

Lemuel Norton
Birth:
Jun. 21, 1785
Edgartown
Dukes County, Massachusetts
Death:
Sep. 18, 1866
Burial:
Hillrest Cemetery
West Tremont, Hancock County, Maine

Son of Noah and Jerusha (Dunham) Norton. (Noah served in Revolutionary War and died in Mass.) He married Mary "Polly" Norton. Rev. Lemuel Norton, was ordained in 1817, in the Calvinist Baptist, but after ten years preaching, changed his views and united with the Freewill Baptist in 1828, and organized a church at Mt. Desert. In 1840, he became pastor of the Belmont Church, and served in the ministry faithfully until his death from cancer of the stomach, at the home of his daughter, Mary. He requested to be "buried on Mt. Desert Island," where he had organized the first Freewill Baptist church in Hancock County, ME.

Rev Chandler Noyes
Birth:
1818
Maine
Death:
Jun. 12, 1878
Waldo County, Maine
Burial:

Highland Cemetery
Jefferson
Lincoln County, Maine

Rev. chandler Noyes, died of consumption. He was the older brother of Rev. Eli Noyes, one of the First Free Baptist missionaries to India, and sons of Moses and Sarah Noyes.

He became a Christian early in life, and at his death had been forty years in the ministry. He preached mostly as an evangelist and saw many revivals. His labors were mostly within the limits of the Montville and Prospect Quarter Meetings. While he had health, he was a faithful worker. He left a devoted wife.-On 14 Nov. 1829, he married Abigail Perkins in Lincoln Co. He married 2) Mary Bailey, 27 Nov. 1843, Johnson, Maine.

Albert Pease
Birth:
Oct. 21, 1811
Norridgewock, Maine
Death:
Jul. 16, 1898
Burial:
Pease Cemetery
Avon
Franklin County, Maine

He came to Christ in 1830 and in 1832 was licensed. In 1843 he was ordained by the Farmington Quarterly Meeting. At first he was an itinerant preacher preaching mostly in Maine. However, thereafter he preached in Massachusetts and Rhode Island, but due to his health he lived with his father in Maine and therefore held many pastorates at the time while his health was poorly. He finally engaged in farming and became a successful writer for agricultural papers. He also wrote the *History Of Phillips*, the city where he lived. He married on February 24, 1830 Ms. Ann Huntoon. His eldest son was a captain of the 17th Regiment New York volunteer's.

Inscription:
"Preacher - Poet - Farmer"

Ezekiel Gilman Page
Birth:
Dec. 25, 1814
New Sharon
Franklin County, Maine
Death:
Jun. 17, 1909
Kennebec County, Maine
Burial:
Litchfield Plains Cemetery
Litchfield Plains
Kennebec County, Maine

His parents were Reuben and Elizabeth (Jackson) Page...He married in March, 1837, Miss Mary G. Bursley, deceased, and has one son living. He married Mrs. Mary Bates, of Oakland, Sept. 12, 1885. He was ordained Dec. 10, 1839" according to "Ordinations" on page 164 of Volume II, Number 1, June 1840, the *Freewill Baptist Quarterly Magazine*. He has been pastor in Edgecomb, Booth Bay (sic), Woolwich, Westport, Brunswick, Georgetown, Richmond Village, West Gardiner, Winnegance, Bowdoinham,

Richmond Corner, Litchfield Plains and West Bowdoin. During his ministry he had charge of two churches at the same time and never without a pastorate or appointment in his 47 years of ministry. Baptized between 400-500, and married 211 couples.

Inscription:
Rev.E. G. Page
Died June 17, 1909
age. 94 yrs.

John Page
Birth:
Feb. 11, 1787
Wentworth
Grafton County, New Hampshire
Death:
Aug. 17, 1834
Garland
Penobscot County, Maine
Burial:
Hathaway Cemetery
Garland
Penobscot County, Maine

He was converted in 1805 and began to preach in 1808. On March 20 of that year he was married by the Rev. Hezekiah Buzzell to Susan Clark and moved to Alton where he served the church at East Bridge. He was ordained they are in 1811 and was pastor of the church 12 years engaging at the same time successfully as an evangelist in the country around assisting in the organization of several churches. In 1820 he moved Maine and begin preaching in that area and organized a church at Garland where he was the pastor for 10 years.

Inscription:
That gospel he preached for twenty two years triumphantly supported him in the hour of death

Page, Rev. John, was born in Wentworth, N. H., Feb. 11, 1787. He removed early in life to Gilmanton, where he was converted in 1805. He began to preach in 1808. March 20 of that year he was married by Rev. Hezekiah Buzzell to Susan Clark, and moved to Alton, where he served the church at East Bridge. He was ordained here in 1811, and was pastor of the church twelve years, engaging at the same time successfully as an evangelist in the country around, and assisting in the organization of several churches. In the winter of 1823–24 he removed to Maine. and began preaching at Corinna and Exeter, but settled in Garland in 1825, where a church was organized, and he had a pastorate for ten years. He labored extensively in revivals in the neighboring town. While on an errand of mercy in 1832 he was severely chilled by a rain, and took a severe cold, which ended in consumption. He died Aug. 17, 1834, in his 48th year. He was a man of robust health and commanding appearance, and his upright life gave power to his words, which were especially blessed in the winning of souls.

William Paine

Birth:
Nov. 19, 1760
Woolwich
Sagadahoc County, Maine
Death:
Oct. 14, 1846
North Anson
Somerset County, Maine
Burial:
Gray Cemetery
Embden
Somerset County, Maine

He was converted under the preaching of Reverent Edward Locke after which he joined the Free Baptist Church. Two years later his wife was converted and united with the church. He was ordained as a minister in the Anson church in October, 1808, with which he remained till death. He was a husband for 60 years and the father of 15 children. He fought in the Revolutionary War as a private in Capt. Wiley's company, Col. Michael Jackson's regiment in 1777. He enlisted at age of 17 and served about three years. Lived in North Anson, Maine. A son of John Payne. A headstone marks his grave. Ref: *Daughters of the American Revolution Magazine, Vol 36 January-June, 1910*

Rev George Parcher

Birth:
Sep. 18, 1781
Saco
York County
Maine
Death:
Jan. 8, 1834
Maine

Burial:
Laurel Hill Cemetery
Saco
York County
Maine

An early Maine Freewill Bapt. minister, said that he was "an ornament to his profession."

Rev Thomas Park

Birth:
Jun. 24, 1795
Maine
Death:
Feb. 23, 1882
Burial:
Bowditch Cemetery
Searsport
Waldo County
Maine

From his bio in "Cyclopedia of Free Baptists," pub. 1889, he was ordained in 1823, and ministered in Maine.

Benjamin P Parker

Birth:
May 16, 1835
Kittery, Maine
Death:
Aug. 3, 1924
Burial:
Hillside Cemetery
North Berwick
York County, Maine

His father was ordained as a Christian minister about 1867. When he was about two years of age, his parents moved to Newburyport, Massachusetts, where his early life was spent in study in the public schools. He was converted on April 18, 1852 and on his 17th birthday was baptized by Rev. Daniel Pike, joining the Christian church there. In the spring of 1859 he united with the First Baptist Church at Greenwood, Maine and on June 2, was licensed at the Otisfield Quarterly Meeting. His first pastorate was at New Gloucester, Maine; in 1862 he moved to Kittery, his birthplace, and was employed at the Navy Yard for six years. Thereafter, he held a number of pastorates in Maine, New Hampshire and Vermont.

He was the first vice president of the Maine Home Mission Society, clerk of the Strafford, Vermont Quarterly Meeting and attended one of the General Conferences.

Rev Alfred Patterson

Birth:
Oct. 5, 1808
Maine
Death:
Mar. 22, 1875
Exeter, NH
New Hampshire
Burial:
Gilman Cemetery
Sangerville
Piscataquis County
Maine
Plot: Row 2 Lot 5

Ordained in March 1839, by Free Will Baptist Sebec Quarterly Meeting. He continued to preach until just before his death cause by heart disease. He Left the denomination and joined the Free Christian Baptists in Cambridge. He was married to Mary P. Gilman.

Rev Charles Sumner Perkins
Birth:
Oct. 25, 1836
Auburn
Androscoggin County
Maine
Death:
Oct. 11, 1905
Maine
Burial:
Riverside Cemetery
Lewiston
Androscoggin County
Maine
Plot: 0845

Rev. Charles Sumner PERKINS, son of Rev. Gideon and Mary (Dunham) Perkins. He prepared for college at the Lewiston Falls Academy, Auburn; graduated from Bowdoin College in 1860, and from Bangor Theological Seminary in 1864.

He became a Christian in 1857, was licensed by the Bowdoin Quarterly Meeting in 1863, by a council of Rev's J.A. Lowell; J. Mariner; C.F.Penney, and D.M. Graham. After his graduation from the theological seminary, he supplied the Free Baptist church in New York City one year; then in 1865-66 he supplied the Roger Williams church, Providence, nearly a year,

during the absence of Dr. Day. In this year his labors were rewarded with nearly one hundred conversions. His first settlement was with the Park Street church, Providence. During this pastorate of six years the church was reorganized, its location changed from N. Main St., and the present edifice on Park St. was built. He then became pastor of Greenfield, R.I., over two yrs, and next of the Portland, ME church five years. Then he was called to the Boston church, Mass. He remained six years and secured the permanent establishment of the church in its present location on Shawmut Ave. He was pastor of the church at Lyndon Centre, VT. He has baptized over two hundred persons.

He has held several public and denominational positions as recording and corresponding secretary of the Foreign Mission Society, member of the Foreign Mission and Home Mission Boards, also of the executive committee of these and of the Education Society, overseer of Bates College, and member of four General Conferences. He is superintendent of schools in Lyndon Centre. He married Nov. 30, 1864, Mary S. Murray, of Brunswick, ME. Their oldest son, Albert T., graduated from Harvard, class of 1887. Martha graduated from the Lyndon Institute in 1886. Osborn in the latter school.

Rev Gideon Perkins
Birth:
Nov. 28, 1801
Woodstock
Oxford County,Maine
Death:
Jan. 25, 1884
Lewiston
Androscoggin County, Maine
Burial:
Riverside Cemetery
Lewiston
Androscoggin County, Maine
Plot: 0362

Rev. Gideon Perkins resided in his native town until after he entered the ministry. His father, Cornelius Perkins, was one of the earliest settlers of the town, having come from Carver, Mass, when he was a young man. A devoted Christian and a deacon in the Baptist church, he brought up his children in the fear of the Lord and saw all eight of them converted. Three became preachers, Gideon was one. His opportunities for education were very limited, but he made the most of them, gaining information easily by natural aptitude, where most young men would have remained ignorant. He was converted at the age of thirty and was baptized by Rev. Aaron Fuller. Previous to his conversion he had married Mary Dunham--a most worthy and helpful Christian wife through life---and had settled on a farm.

His conviction was to preach the gospel and he very soon began to hold meetings. His license to preach is dated Aug. 21, 1831, and is signed by Andrew Hobson, Clerk of then Gorham Q.M. He was ordained Sept. 27, 1832, by Rev's Joseph Hutchinson, Clement Phinney and James Libby. Clement Phinney preached the sermon, and according to the testimony of an eye witness, he preached upon his knees, mingling his words of address to the people with petitions to God.

Like all our ministers of that period Mr. Perkins traveled much from place to place; but he was located for considerable periods in Otisfield, Hebron, Bridgton, Danville, W. Gardiner, Wayne, and Sabattsville. He had everywhere marked sucess. Upon his own testimony not less than two thousand were converted under his preaching, of whom twenty-seven entered the ministry. During his pioneer ministry his salary was seldom sufficient.

He was a man of fine natural ability and of excellent acquirements. He was a good preacher, thoughtful, clear, earnest, tender and persuasive. He was especially gifted in prayer. When he prayed everybody felt that he was speaking to God, and that he was really bringing those for whom he prayed into God's very presence.

He was among the first in Maine to espouse the anti-slavery and temperance causes. He was the first abolitionist sent to the State Legislature by the town of Lewiston. His home was a rendezvous for anti-slavery lecturers and escaped slaves. He was often threatened with violence, but escaped personal injury.

One of his children, John W. Perkins, was one of the most prominent both in counsels and benefactions among the founders of the Maine State Seminary (now Bates College). Another is the Rev. Charles S. Perkins, and another Miss Sarah A. Perkins. In the home of another son, Joseph W. Perkins, many years a merchant in Lewiston, he passed away peacefully and trustfully"

What A Day That Will Be When My Saviour I Shall See!

Seth W Perkins
Birth:
Aug. 26, 1810
Death:
Jun. 14, 1881
Hollis,
Me.
Burial:
Riverside Cemetery
Dixfield,
Oxford County,
Maine

About the year 1866 he settled in South 'Wheelock, Vt., and remained three years; then he was pastor of the Eaton and Newport church, Province of Quebec, three years. After this he was pastor one year in each of the following places in Maine: Canton, Wiltoll, Weld, New Sharon, South Montville and New Gloucester.

Rev John Pettengill
Birth:
Feb. 7, 1834
Sandwich, Carroll County
New Hampshire
Death:
1919
Maine
Burial:
Fairview Cemetery
Jefferson
Lincoln County, Maine

Clement Phinney
Birth:
Aug. 16, 1780
Death:
Mar. 2, 1855
Burial:
Western Cemetery,
Portland
Cumberland County,
Maine

Rev. John Pettengill, son of John and Sally (Hatch) Pettingill was converted at the age of twenty-three. He received license to preach in 1861, and was ordained Jan. 17, 1875. His pastorates have been in North Lisbon, Jackson, Thronton Gore, East Holderness, Moltonboro, Eaton, NH, and South Gorham and Scarboro, ME, where he preached in 1887. Leaving the latter interest in 1888, he took in its place the South Buxton church. He has had hundreds of conversions in his ministry.

He married in 1855, Miss Laura A. Read, and has two children [1889]. Rev. John married Fannie Wescott 11 Sept 1894, at Portland, ME.

He became a minister in the early 1800's. He served at the Free Will Baptist Church, Standish, Maine from 1816-1825. Had a talent for singing, and frequently used it in meetings and at school. He had an unusual wit, won many friends and could hold the undivided attention of large audiences. A book on his life was written by D.M. Graham.

Joseph Phinney
Birth:
Unknown
Death:
December 3, 1869
Harrison, Maine
Burial:
Saint John Cemetery
Pembroke
Washington County, Maine

He died in his 81st year and for many years he preached the gospel with a particular power and success until he was trouble with ill health.

John Pike

Birth:
Aug. 25, 1793
Cornish,York County, Maine
Death:
Nov. 29, 1877
East Fryeburg
Oxford County, Maine
Burial:
Pike Cemetery
Fryeburg, Oxford County, Maine

He was the son of John and Nancy (Thurston) Pike He married Hannah (Hubbard) Pike March 23, 1819, East Fryeburg, Oxford County, Maine. He was in the ministry about fifty years, and preached in Fryeburgh, Brownfield, Harrison, Chatham, Conway, Sweden, Hiram and Sebago. He usually preached to more than one church at a time. His ministry was successful in the conversion of souls. In his former years he did much justice and probate business. He was an earnest advocate of reforms, including abstinence from tobacco.
Inscription:
Age: 84 yrs, 3 mos

The dead in Christ will rise first.

John Pinkham

Birth:
Jan. 25, 1808
Death:
Jan. 18, 1882
Burial:
Cook Pinkham Cemetery, Casco,
Cumberland County, Maine

He was converted at the age of sixteell and joined the church. When about eighteen years of age, he began to hold meetings in his own and adjoining towns with good results. At the request of his church the Q. M. licensed him. In 1830, at the age of twenty-two, he was ordained in Freedom, N. H. His pastorates were, Sandwich seven years, Gilford eight years, and Alton five years. He lived at Dover two years, and preached as an evangelist at Great Falls and Portsmouth. In the latter place a Church was organized. His health became impaired so that he ceased to preach. He then moved to Casco, Me., and cared for his aged parents while they lived. As soon as health permitted he entered into the work again and preached to churches in the Otisfield and Cumberland Q. M's. As formerly, his labors were very fruitful. The Second Poland church, of which he was a member when he died, held him in high esteem, as did also the community in which he lived.

Inscription:
REV JOHN PINKHAM
BORN
JAN 25 1808
DIED JAN 8 1892
Rest, sweet rest

Rev Orrin Pitts
Birth:
Unknown
Sidney
Kennebec County,Maine
Death:
Nov. 18, 1884
Gilmanton Ironworks
Belknap County
New Hampshire
Burial:
Riverside Cemetery
Farmington
Franklin County,Maine

His father died when he was three years old, and he lived with Mr.

Joseph Butterfield, of West Farmington, ME until his twenty-first year, when he began a course of three years at the Farmington Academy, during which he was employed as assistant teacher and lived in the family of the preceptor. He taught about forty-five terms of school several of them in high schools, and continued his work as an educator till near the close of his life.

At the age of thirty-two he was converted, and not long after united with the church in New Portland (Free Baptist).

He was a licentiate one year and then was ordained by the Anson Quarterly Meeting, June 9, 1861. He preached in a number of places in the Anson Q.M; then in 1862, he moved to West Farmington, and lived there six years where he preached in Farmington Falls, New Sharon, and Bean's Corner, where he witnessed a good revival.

After going to Weld with Rev. R. Ely, where they witness a good revival he was soon called to settle there, and remained six years.

A good house of worship was built and many added to the church.

He was twice elected delegate to General Conference.

There is no sting when you die in the Lord.

Albert Pratt
Birth:
unknown
Death:
Oct. 19, 1886
Sebec, Maine
Burial:
Foss Cemetery
Piscataquis County, Maine

He was converted it to age of 31 and was baptized for the Reverend E. Harding on his 32nd birthday and united with the Sebec church. Three years after, in 1856, he was licensed by the Sebec Quarterly Meeting and at the next annual session was ordained. He preached several years, mostly within the limits of this quarterly meeting with good success.

George Plummer
Birth:
Apr. 7, 1826
Durham
Androscoggin County,
Maine
Death:
Jun. 17, 1897
Lisbon Falls
Androscoggin County,
Maine
Burial:
Hillside Cemetery
Lisbon Falls
Androscoggin County,
Maine

He was the son of Henry and Wealthy (Estes) Plummer. He was licensed to preach in the Free Baptist Church, March 1856, and ordained 22 Dec. 1861.He was pastor in Durham five years, at Lisbon Falls five years, at Freeport one year and W. Bowdoin one year. He baptized 60, married 190 couples, and attended 636 funerals. He was a Member of Maine Legislature in 1859.

Rev Benaiah Pratt
Birth:
Mar. 4, 1773
Plymouth County
Massachusetts
Death:
Aug. 26, 1846
Maine
Burial:

Grove Cemetery
Belfast
Waldo County, Maine

Ordained in 1807, preached all over Maine with success. His first wife d. 1819, and March 10, 1825, he married Rachel Heal. He studied medicine, for support, but preached with any rescued time he had. Attended all meetings, and d. age 73. He org. many churches and baptized about 500 person Very successful Freewill Baptist minister, in Maine, where in abt 1816, Topsham, Bristol and Woolwich, he preached 3 times daily for three wks.' with over 100 conversions.

Rev Cyprian S Pratt
Birth:
Aug. 14, 1806
Hebron
Oxford County
Maine
Death:
Jul. 8, 1858
Harmony
Somerset County, Maine
Burial:
Libby Cemetery
Harmony
Somerset County, Maine
Maine Records: His parents were William and Martha (unk) Pratt. He was converted about the year 1831, on Fox Island, and subsequently joined the Free Baptists. Licensed by the Exeter Quarterly Meeting (QM) in Brighton, he devoted several years to an itinerant ministry. After the organization of the Wellington QM,

his labors were confined mostly to its limits.
His health failed while preaching at Richmond. He soon after moved to Harmony and engaged in secular pursuits for five years, when consumption caused his decease.. He married Lovina H. Whittier 10 Jan. 1828, at Brighton, ME.

Henry Preble
Birth:
January 9, 1815
Norridgewock,
Maine
Death:
May 5, 1892
Burial:
Maplewood Cemetery
Fairfield
Somerset County, Maine

He was licensed to preach in 1841 and was ordained the next year. For some years he was an evangelist in the Farmington Quarterly Meeting. For nearly 20 years he spent his time pastoring within this body. Thereafter, he labored in the Anson Quarterly Meeting and the Bowdoin Quarterly Meeting as well. He organized a number of churches within the confines of these associations. During his ministry of 46 years he has traveled over 80,000 miles with his own team, not having received as much as four cents a mile for his services. But he served over 40 churches and hundreds were converted and baptized. He was firm in moral reforms and genuine in his loyalty to his denomination.

Nehemiah Preble

Birth:
Sep. 15, 1819
Death:
Jan. 6, 1891
Waterville,
Maine
Burial:
Litchfield Plains Cemetery,
Litchfield Plains,
Kennebec
County,
Maine

In 1849, he was ordained to the gospel ministry in the Free Will Baptist church. He labored with remarkable results wherein many hundreds were converted and baptized. He was much loved and very successful as a pastor, having held that position in the Free Baptist churches in Gardiner, Manchester, West Gardiner, Richmond Corner, Bowdoinham and Litchfield Plains. Of the last mentioned church, he was pastor for eighteen years. In Litchfield, where a large portion of his work was accomplished, he is held in loving remembrance by hosts of friends who recall his faithful labors. Elder Preble was a residence in the town of Richmond for nearly half a century.

Elijah H Prescott

Birth:
Feb. 14, 1831
Death:
Sep. 14, 1872
Burial:
Whitaker Cemetery

Albion
Kennebec County, Maine,

Rev. Elijah H. Prescott was a Free Will Baptist minister, noted in the History of the town. He pastored Candia Village, NH FWB church.

Albert W Purinton

Birth:
Jun. 2, 1811
Bowdoin, Sagadahoc County,
Maine
Death:
May 10, 1878
Maine
Burial:
West Bowdoin Cemetery
West Bowdoin,
Sagadahoc County, Maine

He was the oldest son of Rev. Nathaniel Purinton. He became a Christian when about twenty-two years, influenced by a sermon of Rev. Joseph White. He was baptized by his father and joined the Second Lisbon church, where he was elected a deacon. After a great struggle, he consented to preach, and was licensed by the

Quarterly Meeting in 1841. He preached first to his own church and in other places in his own and adjoining towns. His labors were fruitful, and Jan. 8, 1843, he was ordained. His pastorates were E. Bowdoin, Freeport, two years; Sabattusville, Freeport a second time six years, Bowdoin in all nine years, and Woolwich five years. In 1865 he returned to his native place, where his wife and two daughters died. He then became pastor at Bath four years and afterwards settled at Lisbon, where at the close of an address on Decoration Day in the cemetery, May 30, 1874, he was stricken with paralysis, and after four years of patient waiting he passed to be with his Saviour. In all his pastorates he had marked religious interest, and at Freeport and Bath, houses of worship were build. His second wife, who had faithfully cared for him, was called away seven months before his death

Charles W Purinton
Birth:
Apr. 27, 1849
Bowdoin, Sagadahoc County, Maine
Death:
Oct. 21, 1910
West Bowdoin, Sagadahoc County, Maine
Burial:
West Bowdoin Cemetery
West Bowdoin, Sagadahoc County, Maine

He became a Christian at the age of 15 and graduated from state normal school in 1870 and was a student at Lewiston, Maine for three years. In March 1875 he was licensed by that Bowdoin quarterly meeting and on December 27, 1877 he was ordained. He was a member of the General Conference in 1880 and on October 4, 1882 he married Hattie Newman. He pastored churches in the area.His father was Joseph C. PURINTON, and his mother was Octavia,

Humphrey Purinton
Birth:
Aug. 16, 1758
Bath, Sagadahoc County, Maine
Death:
Jan. 25, 1832
Bowdoin, Sagadahoc County, Maine
Burial:
Old Bowdoin Cemetery
Sagadahoc County, Maine

He was converted at 17 uniting with the Congregationalists at Harpswell. He was a Revolutionary War Patriot from Prov. of Maine serving during 1 Jul 1775-31 Dec. 1777. After his service in the war of the Revolution, in about 1779, he settled in Bowdoin, then a wilderness. He was active in supporting divine worship, and preached some. It became evident that an Arminian element existed in the Baptist church. In the separation which occurred, Bro. Purinton and others united under the name of "Christian Band." Through his ministry large accessions occurred. When the Freewill Baptist movement reached Bowdoin, Purington and his followers joined them. He was ordained in December, 1807. His labors were especially blessed as a revivalist. Finally, with mind bright and soul tranquil, he fell asleep in his 75th year. He was married to Thankful Snow, and they had a large family. Many of his descendants were ministers, deacons and workers in the Free Baptist Church, especially, the West Bowdoin Free Baptist, Bowdoin, ME.

Nathaniel Purinton
Birth:
Aug. 20, 1787
Maine
Death:
Jun. 12, 1862
Bowdoin, Sagadahoc County, Maine
Burial:
West Bowdoin Cemetery
West Bowdoin,
Sagadahoc County, Maine
First pastor of West Bowdoin Free Baptist church. Ordained June 4, 1818. Rev. Nathaniel Purinton was the son of Rev. Humphrey Purinton and Thankful Snow. He was converted in December 1808, when he entered at once upon a

faithful Christian life. He commenced a membership for life with the Second Lisbon church at its organization in May, 1818, and the next month he was ordained as its pastor. This relation he sustained till death with but slight interruptions. He was married to Pricilla Wilson, 20 Sept. 1810, Lincoln, ME.

He was frequently absent to serve destitute churches, and sometimes had two or three under his pastoral care. He possessed a discerning mind, clearness of utterance, a warm, true heart, and was progressive in regard to the benevolent enterprises of his day.

He was constant in his attendance of the Quarterly Meetings, and was frequently engaged on ordination councils and at church organizations. At times he took up the mason's trowel (He was a mason by trade) to enable him to preach the gospel to the poor. He died respected and beloved. One son (Rev. A. W. Purinton), one brother and two nephews entered the Free Baptist ministry.

Constant Quinnam
Birth:
Feb. 9,1807
Wiscasset, Me.
Death:
Apr. 24, 1865
Bowdoinham, Me.
Burial:
Ridge Road Cemetery
Bowdoinham,
Sagadahoc County, Maine

At the age of eighteen, while listening to Rev. E. Hutchins, he decided to accept Christ and was baptized by Hutchins. The woe rested upon him by day and by night, at home and abroad, till he began to preach. He was licensed by the Edgecomb Q. M., Jan. 16, 1830, and was ordained in Whitefield, N. H., Nov. 17, 1831. After an itinerant ministry of several years, during which he saw many converted, teaching school frequently at the same time, he settled as pastor. He was one year each in Georgetown, Booth Bay, Harpswell, Waterville, Hallowell, Richmond and Bowdoin. In 1851 he was pastor of the interest at Litchfield, till in 1855 he entered upon a pastorate at Bowdoinham Ridge which terminated with his death some ten years later. He had good natural abilities, rendered efficient by a good academical training. For several years he served on school committees, and represented both Litchfield and Bowdoinham in the State Legislature. Spouses: Betsey Quinnam (1807 - 1835), & Sarah Swett Quinnam (1809 - 1893).

John Holmes Rand
Birth:
Aug. 3, 1838
Parsonfield,
Maine
Death:
Nov. 7, 1907
Burial:
Riverside Cemetery
Lewiston
Androscoggin County,
Maine

He was a nephew of Rev. James Rand and was fitted for college at Limerick Academy, Parsonfield Seminary and Maine State Seminary. He was a member the first class of Bates College, graduating in 1867. He at once became a teacher of mathematics and of mental and moral philosophy in the New Hampton Institution and continued in that position until 1876 when he was elected to the professorship of mathematics at Bates College. In 1868, he made a public profession of religion and united with the Free Baptist Church at East Parsonfield, Maine. He was married on November 24, 1881 Miss Emma J. Clark of Lewiston a graduate of Bates College in the class of 1881.

Walter Eugene Ranger
Birth:
Nov. 22, 1855.
Wilton,
Maine
Death:
Nov. 4, 1941
Burial:
Evergreen Cemetery
Portland
Cumberland County
Maine
Plot: Sec-I Lot-152 Grv-1

Prof. Walter E. Ranger, son of Peter and Eliza (Smith) Ranger graduated from Wilton Academy, and from Bates College in 1879. He taught in Nichols Latin School. In 1883, he became principal of Lyndon Centre Institute. He has been an earnest worker for Christ. During the past five years as opportunities have sought him, he as delivered sixty sermons and addresses, supplying the Congregational pulpit at one time at Lyndonville, VT, for three months. He labored in the revival of 1885-86, when eighteen students of the Institute found Christ. During five years at the school some fifty have been converted.

Appleton W Reed
Birth:
Jul. 16, 1821
Albion, Maine
Death:
1911
Burial:
Whitaker Cemetery
Albion
Kennebec County, Maine

He was a student at read to feel Seminary. Converted in August, 1835 he was sliced Sunday in 1840, and ordained that Skowhegan, February 8, 1843. He was for 20 years pastor of the Christian denomination and has been 20 years pastor with the Free Baptists. His pastorates were in New Hampshire and Maine.

John N Rines
Birth:
Apr. 3, 1807
Maine
Death:
Dec. 16, 1874
South Thomaston
Knox County,
Maine
Burial:

Pine Grove Cemetery,
Appleton,
Knox County,
Maine

Rines was married to Mercy Dunham (Pease), daughter of James PEASE and Abigail Dunham. He became a Christian when about twenty-six years, and after a long struggle with duty, he entered the ministry. His fields of labor were Lincolnshire, Dixmont, Plymouth, Carmel, Mt. Desert, Thorndike, Brooks, Montville, Monroe, Waldo, ME. He had great success in most of these places. About 1859 his health failed after which he preached only occasionally. He was an earnest and effective speaker, and a devoted Christian.

Joseph Robinson
Birth:
1774
Death:
Mar. 3, 1858
Burial:
Litchfield Plains Cemetery
Litchfield Plains
Kennebec County, Maine

He was ordained in Maine in 1818. After of which he assisted in many of the churches and revival seem to follow him in most places he went in Maine.

Andrew Rollins
Birth:
Sep. 5, 1799,
Topsham, Maine
Death:
Aug. 15, 1859
Burial:
Growstown Cemetery
Brunswick
Cumberland County, Maine

Feeling a call to the ministry in January 1821, he went into the Sandy River country and began holding meetings, and the next year he was ordained by the Gorham Quarterly Meeting at Danville, and had a useful itinerant ministry of eighteen or twenty years.On May 17 1829, he married Miss Huldah Freeman. He accepted a call to Brunswick, and a revival at once beginning over one hundred were baptized. Some four years later, in a protracted meeting of twenty-one days, assisted by Rev. Clement Phinney, he saw another revival in which a hundred were baptized, mostly among the young. In 1841 he became pastor of the church at Topsham, and after two or three years returned to his itinerant ministry. He journeyed preaching through southern New England.

John Alvin Rogers
Birth:
Apr. 29, 1830
Ossipee
Carroll County, New Hampshire
Death:
Feb. 6, 1866
West Newfield, York County, Maine
Burial:
Rogers Family Graveyard
York County, Maine

He was baptized at Lowell, Massachusetts by Rev. A. K. Moulton. At the age of 22 with his family he moved to West Newfield where he married Miss Julia Nealey in 1854. In June 1863, he was licensed up by the Parsonfield Quarterly Meeting. He was ordained at is home on June 21, 1864.

Varnum S Rose
Birth:
Nov. 23, 1810
Islesboro, Maine
Death:
Dec. 14, 1865
Burial:
Islesboro Cemetery #2
Islesboro, Waldo County, Maine

Converted at the age of seventeen, he united with the Baptist church. Ten years later, feeling called to the ministry, on the ground of doctrine he united with the Free Baptists and in 1831 was ordained. He moved later to Monroe on the mainland, seeking for greater usefulness.

Rev Ashmun T Salley
Birth:
Sep. 16, 1848
Madison
Somerset County
Maine, USA
Death:

May 21, 1931
Burial:
Riverside Cemetery
Lewiston
Androscoggin County
Maine, USA
Plot: 1152E

Rev. Ashmun T. Salley, was born of Christian parents, richer in the grace of God than in the wealth of the world.

He completed his preparatory studies at Maine Central Institute, and overcoming many obstacles, graduated at Bates college in the class of 1875. Having been converted two years preceding his entrance into college, he worked as a Christian student accepting a call to the ministry of the gospel. After teaching one year at Lapham Institute, R.I., he returned to Bates College, graduating from the Theological School in 1879. While yet a student he supplied the church at Lawrence, Mass., for a time, and later the Roger Williams church of Providence, R.I., and he was ordained pastor of the latter church in the fall of 1879. He continued in this relation, doinig useful substantial work, until called to the chair of Sacred Literature at Hillsdale College, Mich. in 1883, which position he filled acceptably. He was invited the same year to supply the Hillsdale College church. These double duties not proving too arduous for him.

On 18 Aug. 1880, he married Miss Ellen Clark, sister to Mrs. John H. Rand, and two children now bless their home.

Nathaniel Kennard Sargent
Birth:
Mar. 23, 1797
Wells
York County, Maine
Death:
Jan. 13, 1876
Kennebunk
York County, Maine
Burial:
Hope Cemetery
Kennebunk, York County, Maine

He was born in the southern part of Wells, and was married Sept. 17, 1818, to Miss Susan Brooks, of Sanford, with whom he lived fifty-four years. He moved to Wells Beach in 1826, became a Christian in 1827, and united with the church in that place. He was ordained at Acton June 8, 1837, by Samuel Burbank and others. In the same year he moved to Kennebunk, and was one year pastor of the church. After this, he preached as he had opportunity in destitute places. He was clerk of the York County Q. M. four years. He was a pioneer in the temperance and anti-slavery causes.

His zeal, conscientiousness and sterling integrity gave him influence in these enterprises. He was appointed collector of customs by President Lincoln in 1861, and held the office till 1875.His wife Susan is recorded as being blind. He was the son of William SARGENT{born - 2 June 1752 at York, Maine who died - 13 November 1824 at Wells, York, Maine Occupation - Farmer; Owner of schooner 'Elmira' Served in the Revolutionary War}. and wife Susannah ALLEN {born - 26 March 1757at York, York, Maine}.

Inscription:
NATHL. K. SARGENT
died January 13, 1876
aged 78 years 10 months.

Edward Savage
Birth:
Nov. 21, 1766
Woolwich
Sagadahoc County, Maine
Death:
Aug. 27, 1856
Solon
Somerset County, Maine
Burial:
Murphy Cemetery
Embden
Somerset County, Maine

Reverend' Edward Savage moved to Embden, where he was converted in March 1789, and was baptized the same month, being the first person baptized in Seven Mile Brook. A church was organized at Anson in August and united with the Farmington Quarterly Meeting. In 1801, he was ordained, and was devoted to the spiritual welfare of his people and deeply interested in all the benevolent causes of the day.In June 1838, he removed his standing to the Embden and Concord church. He died in his 90th year at the residence ofhis son, at Solon, Maine. Edward and Sarah married on 8 June 1790 at Woolwich, Sagadahoc, Maine left thirten children, seventy-five grandchildren and twenty-five great-grandchildren.

There is no sting when you die in the Lord.

Rev Ebenezer Scales
Birth:
Nov. 6, 1766
Nottingham
Rockingham County
New Hampshire
Death:
Feb. 18, 1855
Wilton
Franklin County
Maine
Burial:
Wilton Old Town Cemetery
Wilton
Franklin County
Maine

He had been converted and licensed to preach whenin1803 he moved to Farmington, Me. On Oct 21 1804 he was ordained by the Quarterly Meeting at Anson, Me, preaching his own ordination service. He moved to Wilton, Me., in 1805. He endured many inconveniences traveling to and breaking the bread of life with settlers. His hard labors provided enough property to support and educate a family of eleven children. He was useful in promoting revivals and establishing churches.

At the August Q M in Farmington, in the barn of Rev Asa Libby, he preached the Sabbath in company with Moses Dudley. At the Yearly Meeting at Weare, NH, in 1821, he preached with Rev's John Buzzell and Clarissa H Danforth. A revival followed and sixty were converted. In 1828, he preached at the Rhode Island QM.

He possessed a strong mind, good native talent and spoke with boldness and energy. When the Biblical School was established he looked upon it's success with pleasure and was one of many friends who gave $100 for it's endowment.

Stricken with paralysis he lay for over a year waiting for the summons that would set him free.

Sargent Shaw
Birth:
Dec. 16, 1791
Standish, Me.
Death:
Mar. 4, 1866
Burial:
White Rock Cemetery
White Rock, Cumberland County,
Maine

His father left Congregational church for the Free Baptist church, and he early became acquainted with Randall, Tingley, Buzzell and Stinchfield, as they made his father's house their home. In the revival of 1808-09 in Standish, in which Z. Jordan, A. Files, C. Phinney and J. White found the Saviour, he was converted. After deferring his call to the ministry for years, he was ordained in September, 1828, through the encouragement of Joseph White. He still labored with his hands, preaching as opportunity offered. He was a safe counselor and a true friend to the slave.

Moses Shepard
Birth:
Jan. 18, 1802
New London
Merrimack County
New Hampshire
Death:
Jun. 6, 1860
Bangor
Penobscot County, Maine
Burial:
Mount Hope Cemetery
Bangor
Penobscot County, Maine

He was a clergyman who wanted to preach the gospel in its simplicity, and he went into the wilds of Maine to do so. In 1848, Moses became the guardian to the minor children of Asa Tibbetts of Glenburn, ME. Following his death, Moses' estate was administered by his wife Phebe, and son-in-law Edwin Drew. The birth places of his children given an indication of the various places in which Moses lived and worked: New London, New Hampshire, Sutton, NH, Corinth, Maine, and Hermon, Maine.

This memorialist had an old daguerreotype or tin-type of a man that was not labeled and whose identity was unknown. However, a picture of Moses and his wife Phebe was found in the "History of New London, New Hampshire" and the man pictured in the book was identical to the one in the old framed photo, which is reproduced here.

You Are Home At Last!

Humphrey Small

Birth:
July 26, 1828
Bowdoin, Maine
Death:
1910
Burial:
Rose Cemetery
Brooks
Waldo County, Maine

He was converted when he was 12 years of age and for four years was a member of a Methodist church. He was licensed by the Prospect Quarterly Meeting on June 25, 1858 and then ordained March 10, 1860. He pastored many churches in the area for many years.

James Small

Birth:
1821
Death:
Feb. 26, 1885
Montville, Maine
Burial:
Halldale Cemetery
West Montville
Waldo County, Maine

He accepted Christ as an early age and was baptized by Rev. J. B. Copp and united with the Exeter church. He began to preach at the age of 19 and was ordained in the Exeter Quarterly Meeting. He preached in countless churches during his 45 years of ministry and baptized a large number of converts

Fred Albertis Snow

Birth:
Nov. 23, 1861
North Berwick
York County, Maine
Death:
Oct. 9, 1931
Islesboro
Waldo County, Maine
Burial:
Burr Cemetery
Freeport, Cumberland County,
Maine

Rev. Snow was the first member of his church, the Freewill Baptist Church of North Berwick, to go to divinity school and to be ordained as a Baptist preacher. He went to Colby College, Waterville Maine and later to Newton Seminary, Andover Massachusetts. He was known as a Hebrew and Greek scholar.

Henry F Snow

Birth:
Nov. 25, 1831
Effingham
Carroll County
New Hampshire
Death:
Jan. 1, 1908

Burial:
Riverside Cemetery
Cornish
York County, Maine

He prepared for the ministry at New Hampton Institution and was licensed to preach there. He was ordained 1858 at the Merrimack Street Church, Manchester. Most of his ministry was in Maine but he moved to Tallapoosa, Ga. Devoting most of his time among four colored churches during 1898-1903 before returning back to Effingham Falls where he was to be found in 1908.

He studied at St. Johnsbury Academy. Ordained, Graduated at Bates College, 1874 and Cobb Divinity School 1877. Ordained in North Berwick, Me. 1877. He was the first business manager of the Bates Student. Delegate to the General Conference 1883; member of the Executive Board of the Foreign Missionary society; recording secretary of the Education Society; trustee of Bates College.

Thomas Spooner
Birth:
Feb. 4, 1852
Death:
March 6,1895
Lawrence, Mass.
Burial:
Riverside Cemetery
Lewiston
Androscoggin County, Maine
Plot: 0254W

Elder James Stevens
Birth:
Jun., 1799
Wells
York County
Maine
Death:
Oct. 21, 1886
Boston
Suffolk County
Massachusetts
Burial:
Maple Grove Cemetery
Vassalboro
Kennebec County
Maine

James was a son of Theodore Stevens & Mary Boyd. Older Bro. of Rev. John and Rev. Theodore Stevens,Jr.

Inscription:

Eld.
JAMES STEVENS
DIED
Oct. 21, 1886
AEt. 87ys. 4ms.

Blessed are the dead which
Die in the Lord.

Rev John Stevens
Birth:
Jun. 18, 1801
Maine
Death:
Apr. 5, 1878
Biddeford
York County
Maine
Burial:
Laurel Hill Cemetery
Saco
York County
Maine

He was convinced to preach after his marriage, he having excused himself because of lack of education. But he renewed his covenant and at once his preaching resulted in many conversions. He returned to Limington and taking charge of his father's farm, he labored in the several districts so effectively that the church increased to over three hundred members. He was ordained in June 1823. In 1825, he accompanied

Rev. B.S. Manson, friend from boyhood, on a tour through upper NH and VT to Canada. A collection of $7 was raised in the Parsonfield Q.M. to send them on this mission. He was a member of the second General Conference, held in Sandwich, NH.

Name is in Minutes of 24th General Conference of Freewill Baptists, of 88 ordained ministers who had died since last meeting in Oct. 1877.

Moses Stevens
Birth:
1794
Death:
May 28, 1866
Burial:
West Mills Cemetery
Industry,
Franklin County,
Maine

He was converted in early life, joining the Christian Connection. He united with the Free Baptists from doctrinal preferences, and was licensed *by* the Sebec Q. M. He was ordained in 1832 at Bradford, Me. He joined the Springfield Q. M. at its organization, and for many years was a itinerant ministry.

Rev Theodore Stevens
Birth:
Oct. 10, 1812
Maine
Death:
Oct. 20, 1880
York County
Maine

Burial:
Laurel Hill Cemetery
Saco, York County, Maine

A Free Bapt. ordained minister who labored in Maine. He had two older brothers who were also ministers. Son of Theodore, Sr, and Mary (Boyd) STEVENS. He was mar. to Susan Brackett, 18 March 1836, ME. Their children: Milton T., b. 1845, d. 14 Sep 1911, Waltman, MA; Eunice V., d. 28 Feb. 1868, 24y, 3m.; Theodore Jr. d. 25 June 1862, 20y, 2m, and 15d.Newell T, b. ca 1850 Clara, b. ca 1852, Charles, b.ca 1854; Belle, b.ca 1856; Fanny, b ca 1859.In 1870 census HH was also a dau,Mary Hasty, 33y, with 2 sons, Frank L. age 9, and James E. age 4.

In February, 1877, he was licensed to preach and on June 3, 1880 he was ordained at Milton, Maine by the Otisfield Quarter Meeting. He organized the Carthage church on May 5, 1880 and became it's pastor. He later pastored a number of churches in the area. He was married to Myra C. George and after her passing married on January 30, 1864 to Miss Mary Oldham.

William S Stevenson
Birth:
Feb. 3, 1818
Montville,
Maine
Death:
May 2, 1891
Burial:
Halldale Cemetery
West Montville
Waldo County,
Maine

Freelon Starbird
Birth:
September 14, 1841
Woodstock, Maine
Death:
Jan. 29, 1910
Burial:
Riverside Cemetery
Farmington
Franklin County, Maine

His father, the Col. William Stevenson, was born in Liverpool, England. He was converted at age 13 and joined the church in North Montville. He yielded his call to the ministry in 1868 at the age of 50 and was ordained in June, 1871 at a session of the quarterly meeting at his church. Rev. Ebenezer Knowlton preached the sermon. He has preached mostly as an itinerant and has seen many revivals.

Joseph Stinson
Birth:
October, 1798
Bowdoin, Me.
Death:
Feb. 27, 1864
Burial:
Tilton Corner Cemetery
Pittsfield, Somerset County, Maine

Stinson, Rev. Joseph, son of Rev. William Stinson of the Christian Connection. He married in 1823 Miss· Mary Whittemore, after which for several years he resided in Litchfield, where he was converted and baptized by Rev. S. Hathorn, uniting with the Free

Baptist church there in 1838. In March, 1842, he was ordained by Rev's N. Purington, C. Quinnam and M. Getchell. In 1844 he moved to Pittsfield of the Exeter Q. M., and joined the church there, a relation which continued during life. He served this church with acceptance to their edification. He was deeply interested in the Sunday-school of which he was superintendent.

William C Stinson
Birth:
February 14, 1803
Richmond,
Maine
Death:
Jul. 20, 1886
Pittsfield,
Maine
Burial:
Pittsfield Village Cemetery
Pittsfield
Somerset County,
Maine

He was converted in a revival under Rev. Dexter Waterman. He was ordained in 1857 and in 1861 became pastor away from that area until 1870 when he returned back to Pittsfield where he remained until his death. He was an important factor in the establishment of the Maine Central Institute at Pittsfield. He helped to raise the first $10,000.

Cyrus Stilson
Birth:
1801
Sydney, Maine
Death:
Oct. 17, 1894
Burial:
New Sharon Village Cemetery
New Sharon
Franklin County,
Maine

He was ordained in 1828 and the next year with Leonard Hathaway, entered New Brunswick, Canada, by way of Houlton and for a month preached to large and attentive audiences up and down the St. John's River. At Hodgdon, where a revival was in progress before they arrived, a church was organized and Stilson remained till August. In the meantime making a tour 100 miles further into the Providence where he not only preached but baptized. Age 93 yrs. 7 mo. 25 days at his death.

Alvah Strout
Birth:
Apr. 28, 1810
Limington
York County, Maine
Death:
Aug. 24, 1881
Burial:
Mills Cemetery
Bradford
Penobscot County, Maine
His ministry extended over 45 years and he did much for the cause of Christ in the Sebec Quarterly Meeting.

James Strout, Jr
Birth:
Apr. 24, 1800
Limington
York County, Maine

Death:
Sep. 25, 1878
Exeter Center
Penobscot County, Maine
Burial:
Chamberlain Cemetery
Penobscot County, Maine

Rev. James Strout died in Exeter, ME. At the age of seventeen he was converted but lapsed.While in Harrison he lost his wife and a child, and in his affliction he turned to God. After removing to Bradford, ME, he united with the church in March 1834, and soon began to preach. About 1835 he was licensed, and was ordained in March 1839. He traveled extensively, often on foot, and preached mostly without compensation. He was a workman that needed not to be ashamed. He was a good citizen and elected to offices of trust. He was clerk and treasurer of the Penobscot Yearly Meeting. Though the church where he lived was broken up, he continued a zealous supporter of the denomination. His health and hearing failed a few years before his death.

Elder Nathaniel Sturgis

Birth:
Sep. 3, 1774
Gorham
Cumberland County
Maine
Death:
Oct. 29, 1825
Pejepscot
Sagadahoc County

MaineBurial:
Fitz Cemetery
Auburn
Androscoggin County
Maine

Elder Nathaniel Sturgis, while sick abed in 1801, thinking he would die, became a Christian and later entered the ministry and was ordained 1821, in the Freewill Baptist church. Soon after this, he took a journey of some 400 miles into the British Provinces to preach free salvation.

He was a man of clear mind and strong judgment. He was married to Betsy Woodman 5 Jan. 1806. They had several children, some who died at a young age.

Virgil D Sweetland

Birth:
Sep., 1837
Palmyra,
Maine
Death:
unknown
Burial:
Warren Hill Cemetery
Palmyra
Somerset County,
Maine

His grandfather was a Revolutionary War soldier and a native of Providence Rhode Island. Virgil studied at the Academy and was a member of the First Main Heavy Artillery in the Civil War serving two years. He took part in the desperate charge of May 18, 1864 at Spottsylvania and was wounded. His conversion, which was sudden and radical, occurred in the autumn of 1862. He began to preach in 1876 and was licensed on June 9, 1877 and ordained at Palmyra by Rev's. James Boyd, John Cook, M. H. Tarbox and others on June 18, 1879. He pastored many churches in the area and at one time even pastored four churches at once. He is attended about 200 funerals and married 61 couples. He has been supervisor of schools, the town clerk, and represented his town in the legislature.

David Swett
Birth:
Jun. 22, 1792
Gorham, Me.
Death:
Jul. 13, 1869
Burial:
Libby Hill Cemetery
Albion, Kennebec County, Maine
Plot: row 1

He was ordained in 1822. In the Montville Q. M. in 1824 at Dixmont

and Newburg, he baptized 106 during three months. His ministry was confined to Maine, New Hampshire and Vermont.

Jesse Swett
Birth:
1807
Gorham, Maine
Death:
Mar. 15, 1840
Burial:
Ridge Road Cemetery
Bowdoinham
Sagadahoc County, Maine

He was converted in 1827 and baptized by the Rev. Clement Phinney and united with the church at Windham. In 1828, while in Dover, New Hampshire, with his brother, trying to advance the cause of Christ, he became to consider the duty of the ministry. He already had three brothers in the ministry at that time. He continued to exhort at home until 1830 when he spent some time in Bowdoinham and Litchfield. His work with blessed and in January, 1831 he was licensed by the Gorham quarter Meeting and in June 1832 was ordained by the Bowdoin Quarter Meeting. In September of the following year he formed the Second Richmond church with 15 members and resided there until the spring of 1837 during which time the church and had grown to 50 members. He died at the home of his father-in-all Capt. Sanford in Bowdoinham where his sermon was preached by the Rev. Stephen Purington.

Rev Josiah Spooner Swift
Birth:
Feb. 28, 1813
Wareham
Plymouth County
Massachusetts
Death:
Mar. 26, 1883
Wilton
Franklin County
Maine
Burial:
Riverside Cemetery
Farmington
Franklin County
Maine

Son of Josiah and Eleanor (Spooner) Swift. Married Martha Coney Flint in Sep 1834 at Bath, Maine.

He was a Freewill Baptist minister, an orchardist and nurseryman, and an amateur artist. He is best known as a publisher, characterized as "the father of journalism in Franklin County [Maine].

Bates College in Lewiston, Maine holds his early papers as part of the Edmund S. Muskie Archives and Special Collections Library

---

Bradbury Sylvester
Birth:
Nov. 19, 1815
Leeds,
Maine
Death:
Aug. 31, 1889
Burial:
Evergreen Cemetery
Wayne
Kennebec County, Maine

He was licensed in 1868 and on September 29, 1877 was ordained by the Bowdoin Quarter Meeting.

Rev Moses H Tarbox

Birth:
Sept. 8, 1824,
Kennebunk Port
Maine
Death:
Apr. 13, 1907
Burial:
Riverside Cemetery
Lewiston
Androscoggin County
Maine
Plot: 0442

His parents were Daniel and Susan (Hanscom) TARBOX. He prepared for college at Farmington, ME, and Lewiston Falls Academy, and graduated from Waterville College in 1849, and Bangor Theological Seminary in 1855.

He was ordained by the Kennebec Quarterly Meeting in 1851, and was pastor at Sabattus, ME, three years; at Bangor, ME, seven years, where a house of worship was built, revivals being enjoyed at both these places; at Kendall's Mills, ME, one year; at Amesbury, Mass. three years; at Cornishville, ME, one year; at Dover, ME, four years, and at Houlton, ME, three years. Revivals resulted from his labors at Dover and Houlton, a church being organized at the latter place and a house erected. He was also missionary in the city of Lewiston three years, and in the Penobscot Yearly Meeting for a like period.

Subsequently moving to Minnesota, he became pastor of the Elk River church, and did much to strengthen it.

He was married in 1856 to Adrianna Weymouth, and in 1882, to Mrs. M.E. Nash. He has five children, one of whom, O.C. Tarbox, graduated from Bates College in 1880 and practice medicine in New York City.

Ebenezer Tasker

Birth:
Unknown
Death:
Sep. 24, 1839
Burial:
Mudgett Cemetery
Dixmont
Penobscot County, Maine

Friend D. Tasker

Birth:
Jul. 31, 1850
Jackson, Maine
Death:
Oct. 24, 1904
Burial:
Mount Pleasant Cemetery
Dexter
Penobscot County, Maine

He became a Christian at 28 and on January, 1879 he was licensed, and in December, 1880 was ordained. He held several pastorates in Maine.

Sophia Thomas
Birth:
December 14, 1814
Limerick, Maine
Death:
Jan. 22, 1888
Burial:
Woodlawn Cemetery
Biddeford
York County, Maine

On April 30, 1836 she married Samuel Thomas. She was converted in her childhood and early felt the call to preach. She made a resolute struggle for an education and was greatly interested in God's word. In 1845 she gathered all the Free Will Baptist she could find in Biddeford to her home, where January 15, 1848 a Free Will Baptists church was organized. Her husband became its first Deacon. After many years of devoted ministry she died at her daughter's home.

Thomas W Thompson
Birth:
181
Litchfield
Kennebec County, Maine
Death:
Apr. 26, 1894
Sumner
Oxford County, Maine
Burial:

Fields Hill Cemetery
Oxford County, Maine
His parents were Joel and Rachel (Wilson) Thompson. He became a Christian at the age of eighteen, and was Ordained Freewill Baptist by Rev. C. W. Goule. He had been pastor of the Carthage, Weld, and Livermore churches, and from 1880, of the Summer church. He has organized one church and had three revivals. He was married in 1837 to Miss Hannah Hammond.

Rev Benjamin Thorne
Birth:
Mar. 30, 1779
Cumberland County, Maine
Death:
Dec. 4, 1864
Auburn
Androscoggin County, Maine
Burial:
Herrick Cemetery
Lewiston
Androscoggin County, Maine

Parents: Samuel Thorne and Hannah (Hoyt) Thorne. Married: 1) Alice Dresser, dau of Aaron and Alice Dresser. On Aug. 1804, ME. Bio taken from Eminent Preachers, by Selah H Barrett, and FWB Cyclopedia, pub. 1889.]
Rev. B. Thorne, appears to have been interested in religion at an early age. He listened to the first Freewill Baptist minister, Eld. Benjamin Randall, who preached in Lewiston. Eld Randall's sentiments, doctrine, etc, were embraced by Benjamin, his parents and quite a number of others, and formed

substantially the basis of his life and ministry.

In the year 1800, a few persons with himself were organized into the First Freewill Baptist Church in Lewiston, and in 1809, he was ordained to the gospel ministry. Eld. Thorne was a self-educated man, having very limited educational advantages at that time. He studied, and acquired a commendable knowledge of the Latin and Greek languages, knew something of the Hebrew and mastered the French after he had passed his eightieth year. He was generally prepared to give a satisfactory reason of views he entertained. While his hands were employed in daily toil, his mind was equally industrious upon difficult questions in both theology and philosophy, which enabled him to acquire a larger and more useful fund of knowledge than not-a-few persons acquired.

His ministry was centered in the area round about for over 57 years, and he was the oldest inhabitant of the town at the time of his death with a longer residence than any other person of eighty-five years. He was permitted to see great changes--from a wilderness to cultivated farms; a few log houses displaced for large, convenient ones; a few families grown to a population of eight thousand souls; schools, churches, banks, mills, public buildings, a seminary and at last, Bates College, honoring the town, in which he manifested a lively interest.

The private Christian character of Mr. Thorne was formed by the sterling piety of his mother and Freewill Baptists of those days. His integrity to Christian principles was never questioned. His hospitality and kindness were large and liberal, and honesty was never questioned.

He was one of the best and most talented ministers of his time. His extreme modesty left many unconscious of his superior ability, unless some special occasion made it manifest.

Few persons were ever blessed with a stronger memory, and chapters, if not entire books in the Bible, could be repeated by him verbatim in his last years, and with surprising skill and accuracy. This talent no doubt, was a source of much power.

He had a large family of ten children to support entirely dependent upon his own labors. He did not receive in all his life, one hundred dollars for his services in preaching.

Born in the midst of the Revolutionary War, he imbibed its patriotism until the last. His five grandsons fought in the Civil War.

He labored and enjoyed revivals of religion both in the villages and in his own neighborhood, and never better than in his last days. His vigor of mind and body continued unabated until he looked the age of a sixty-five year-old man, rather than eighty-five. Some of his best discourses were preached only a few days before his death.

His last sickness was short, his work was done and he was ready to depart. Peaceful and trusting he fell asleep on Sabbath eve, Dec. 4,

1864, aged 85yrs, 9m, calm as the setting sun of mid-summer.

He left an aged and infirm widow of eighty-three years, who had been in very deed a most devoted wife and mother for nearly sixty-five years; kind and faithful children, and many grand and great-grandchildren, to mourn their loss. One of the earliest ministers in the Benjamin Randall Freewill Baptist New England church. He was a useful and faithful man. May he be remembered here.

Pelatiah Tingley
Birth:
Jan. 3, 1735
Middlesex County, Massachusetts
Death:
Sep. 3, 1821
Waterboro, York County, Maine
Burial: Woodward/Tingley,
Waterboro, York County, Maine

At age sixteen, he had serious reflections regarding religion and was encouraged to obtain a collegiate education. so he went through the preparatory studies, and in 1757, at the age of twenty-two, entered Yale College, in New Haven, Conn. He graduated in 1761. His class at the time of graduating, consisted of thirty young men, of whom ten afterward became ministers, and one of them, several years later, was chosen governor of the state of Georgia. He heard Rev. Benjamin Randall, founder of the Free Will Baptist in NH, preach and felt he had the same sentiments for a general atonement and other biblical doctrines. He joined that church and was ordained a Free Will Baptist Minister in 1764, which he followed until his death. He was the first FWB minister of Waterboro, ME. On Dec. 26, 1787, the town of Waterboro, voted to send the first representative to the Convention in Boston, to ratify the Constitution. The person they chose was Rev. Pelatiah Tingley. (Some info from *Memoirs of Eminent Preachers in the Freewill Baptist Denomination--1874* by Selah Hibbard Barret

Edward Toothaker
Birth:
May 20, 1813
Bowdoinham
Sagadahoc County, Maine

Death:
Feb. 12, 1879
Rangeley
Franklin County, Maine
Burial:
Evergreen Cemetery
Phillips, Franklin County, Maine

His parents moved to Rangeley when he was eight years of age. He became a Christian and a member of the church there in early life. He began to preach when about twenty-one, and was ordained at the June session of the Farmington Q. M. in 1849. His ministry was mostly within the limits of the Farmington and Ansoil Q. M's. His last pastorate was with the Phillips church. He was highly esteemed by those among whom he had faithfully preached the gospel forty-five years and lived an exemplary Christian life.

Christopher Tracy
Birth:
Oct. 2, 1758
Falmouth,
Cumberland County,
Maine
Death:

Nov. 12, 1839
Burial:
Littlefield Cemetery,
Lisbon Falls,
Androscoggin County,
Maine

Eld. Tracy was baptized by Eld. Benjamin Randall in 1781, and was one of the original members of the Free Baptist Church of Durham, organized 1790, of which he remained a member until his death. He was ordained a minister of the gospel, Aug. 31, 1808, by Elders Ephraim Stinchfield, Adam Eliot, and Benjamin Thorn. Rev. Tracy was an evangelist; a well-read and educated man for his time, of excellent judgment; earnest and forceful as a public speaker. He had four sons who were licensed to preach: Jonathan, Asa, Christopher, Jr., and Daniel.

Etta G Goodwin Tracy
Birth:
Oct. 8, 1865
Kennebec County, Maine
Death:
Oct. 17, 1917

Skowhegan,
Somerset County, Maine
Burial:
Mount Auburn Cemetery,
Auburn,
Androscoggin County, Maine

Etta was the daughter of Charles N. and Emma C. (Ellis) Goodwin, both of Maine. She attended Bates College and became a teacher before she was ordained a minister in 1910. She served churches at So. Berwick, ME; Pittsfield and Meredith Center, N.H. churches. She was a resident of New Hampton, NH.

Olin Hobbs Tracy
Birth:
Jul. 4, 1857
Minot,
Androscoggin County, Maine
Death:
Aug. 7, 1944

Stoneham,
Middlesex County,
Massachusetts
Burial:
Mount Auburn Cemetery,
Auburn,
Androscoggin County, Maine

Olin H. Tracy was the son of Ferdinand Tracy and Sylvia J. (Hobbs) Tracy. (He was grandson of Rev. Jonathan and Abigail (Small) TRACY). He was a resident of Lewiston Maine in 1857, where he attended Nichols Latin School, a preparatory school. He then went to Bates College, Lewiston, where he was graduated in 1882. On 3 Nov. 1884, he married Miss Susan Elizabeth Barbarick, at Ossippee, Carroll Co. NH. He was ordained to the Free Will Baptist ministry on 24 June 1885, by Prof. J. Fullerton, D.D. In 1885, he was graduated from Cobb Divinity School. He moved to Oakland, Alameda Co. CA. after his graduation, and there his wife, Susan died in childbirth in 1891. He moved to Minneapolis, MN, where he was found in 1891. In 1896, he was married to Rev. Etta Gertrude Goodwin, in

Kennebec, ME. (She was not ordained until 1910, some years after her marriage). In 1901, at age 44 years, he was awarded the D.D. degree from Hillsdale College, MI. In 1910, he was a resident in Pittsfield, Merrimack, NH, age 63...probably a pastor. Cem., Auburn, Androscoggin Co. Maine.

Jonathan Tracy
Birth:
Dec. 28, 1782
Durham,
Androscoggin County, Maine
Death:
Jan. 24, 1864
Wales Corner,
Androscoggin County, Maine
Burial:
Mount Auburn Cemetery
Auburn,
Androscoggin County, Maine

Jonathan; Christopher, Jr; Asa, and Daniel. Jonathan and his father, Christopher, Sr., were ordained Free Will Baptist ministers in that part of Maine and did great work. (Hist. of Durham, ME, by Everete Stackpole, Lewiston, 1899.)Rev. Jonathan was named for is grandfather, Jonathan Tracy of

Gouldsboro. It was said he was a good type of his ancestors and showed his Norman origin in his extremely light hair and blue eyes. He had a sturdy and powerful frame, though only of medium height. Rev. Jonathan moved to Minot, now Auburn, when a young man. Ordained 24 Feb. 1828. Was called "Scripture Tracy" for his remarkable familiarity with the Bible. He baptized between 700-800 converts, and one time 45 through a hole cut in the ice. He was an earnest advocate of temperance and anti-slavery. He d. at Wales, aged 81 yrs. The text at his funeral was I Cor. XV 58, "Steadfast and unmovable always abounding in the work of the Lord." Two of his grandsons, Rev. A.P. Tracy of VT and Rev. Olin H. Tracy of Boston, entered the ministry of the Free Bapt. Church.

Rev Isaac Tripp
Birth:
Dec. 14, 1770
Bristol
Lincoln County
Maine
Death:
Sep. 18, 1827
Maine
Burial:
Orchard Hill Cemetery

Temple
Franklin County
Maine

Rev. Isaac Tripp was an early Maine Freewill Bapt. minister, ordained in 182_.

Me Rev Joseph Trueworthy

Birth:
May 12, 1816
Hancock County
Maine
Death:
Oct. 29, 1881
Ellsworth
Hancock County
Maine
Burial:
Dollardstown
Ellsworth
Hancock County,Maine

Rev. Joseph Trueworthy, was the son of Amaziah and Hannah Trueworthy. He married Mrs. Margery Paine (Brown) Dollard, widow of William Dollard, 04 Nov. 1842. She was the dau. of Samuel Hinckley Brown and Margery (Paine) Brown.

Joseph was converted when young and united with the Baptist church in Ellsworth. When he became acquainted with the views of the Free Baptists, he joined the West Ellsworth church, of which he remained a member during life. In 1859 he was licensed by Ellsworth Quarterly Meeting and in March 1862, ws ordained. He spent a few years in Aroostook County, working with his hands and preaching as he was able. The rest of his ministry was within the limits of the Ellsworth QM. He was an earnest worker.

Family Records/genealogy state he and his wife were buried on the Dollard 35-acre estate, in Ellsworth that Margery was willed by her former husband, William Dollard.

Abel Turner

Birth:
14 Mar 1811
Death:
1878
Burial:
South Dover Cemetery
Dover-Foxcroft,
Piscataquis County, Maine
Plot: South Section, Row 9

He moved to Foxtrot, ME, among the early pioneers. Eld.Turner heard of Baptist meetings in the area when a young man, went to hear, and began his life as a Free Will Baptist, rejecting his Calvinistic upbringing. There is a book, *The Life and Travels of Abel Turner, Minister of the Gospel*--Written by himself, Written for his Wife, dated 1839----------"His father, Abel Turner, it said, was born in

Pembroke, Mass, a descendent of John Turner, one who came over with the Pilgrims. He moved to Foxtrot, ME, among the early pioneers, where the last two of his eight children, Adam B., ca 1817, and Betty B, late 1818, were born. Eld. Abel Turner heard of Baptist meetings in the area when a young man, went to hear, and began his life as a FreeWill Baptist, rejecting his Calvinistic upbringing. He was ordained at age 21 yrs, in about 1832. His ministry was in Maine, Vermont, and Western New York. He lived out his life as a FWB preacher in Chester, Penobscot Co. ME.

Matthias Ulmer
Birth:
1809
Death:
Jun. 24, 1878
Appleton, Me.
Burial:
Pine Grove Cemetery
South Montville, Waldo County, Maine

Ulmer died at age 69 years and 9 months. His father died when he was young, and being the oldest, the care of his mother and a large family devolved upon him. He fulfilled his trust well. He early became a Christian and was a pioneer worker in every good cause. He organized the first temperance society in that part of the state, in March, 1828. His bold stand against slavery gave him a prominent position in political matters. He lost a son in the war. His labors were mostly with the people of the Montville Q. M., and for fifty years he spared neither time nor money for their advancement. His fine business talent made him efficient in the management of churches.

Sidney Wakely
Birth:
Oct 7, 1850.
Trowbridge Wiltshire, England
Death:
1937
Burial:
New Village Cemetery
Clinton
Kennebec County, Maine

He came to the United States in 1869, when about eighteen years old. He was converted when sixteen and joined the Wesleyan Methodist church in Trowbridge. He joined the Free Baptist church at Lisbon Fallls, ME, and was baptized by immersion. His early education was in the English Church school. He was licensed by his church Feb. 1, 1879, and by the Bowdoin Quarterly Meeting June 1881, and was ordained at West Poland, Maine, by the Cumberland Quarterly Meeting, Oct. 4, 1882. He was pastor at West Bowdoin over a year, West Poland one year, Casco two years, at the same time a year at East Otisfield, and Bow Lake, N.H., three years. He settled at Kittery Point, Maine, March 1, 1855.He was married Aug. 22, 1870, to Miss Emma White and had eight children.

John B. Wallace
Birth:
Jan. 31, 1787
Mystic, Massachusetts
Death:
Aug. 19, 1851
Freeman
Franklin County, Maine
Burial:
North Freeman Cemetery
Farmington
Franklin County, Maine

After his birth he was carried by his parents the next year to New Brunswick, Canada. In 1809 he experienced religion with the Baptists. Two years later he married a pious lady, and in 1814 he moved to Marmashe. In 1818, having moved to Belgrade, Maine, he became interested in the reformation there prevailing, and joined the Free Baptist Church. In 1830, he moved to Freeman, near the kingfield line, and by his labors a small church was revived and strengthen till it became large and flourishing. August, 1838 he was licensed by the Anson Quarterly Meeting and on May 11, 1845 he was ordained. He helped organized a church in the center of the town of Freeman where he afterwards lived till his death.

Dexter Waterman
Birth:
Jun. 13, 1807
Litchfield, Me.
Death:
Feb. 8, 1890
Burial:
Growstown Cemetery,
Brunswick,
Cumberland County, Maine

In Jan. 1828, he was licensed to preach for the Free Will Baptist. He was ordained in July 1828, by Rev's Robbins, Joseph Robinson, and Silas Curtis, and for six years led an itinerant ministry, witnessing many revivals in the Bowdoin and Edgecomb Q.M's. In the twenty-five churches he served, as many as 375 were converted and baptized. Four churches were organized by his help. He became interested in the temperance and anti-slavery movements, preaching, lecturing and voting; has been two years president of the Foreign Mission Society, a member of the board of corporators of the Printing Establishment since 1844, nine times a delegate to General Conference. He was one of the four brethren that originated the call for the convention that organized the Education Society, Jan. 18, 1840, and joined in the efforts to endow that society. His two winters, of seven months each, at Harper's Ferry, were especially blessed. He is now trustee of Bates College and of Storer College. During more than fifty years of active labors at over eighty years of age he was still active, conducting the preaching service every Sunday, and attending the other meetings of the church.

Elder Samuel Weeks
Birth:
Nov. 21, 1746
Greenland
Rockingham County
New Hampshire
Death:
Jun., 1832
Parsonsfield
York County, Maine
Burial:
East Parsonsfield Cemetery
Parsonsfield
York County, Maine

Rev. Samuel, son of Matthias and Sarah (Sanborn-Ford) Weeks. In February, 1783, he removed from Gilmanton to Parsonsfield, and soon afterward began preaching there and elsewhere in that vicinity. With the assistance of Elder Randall he organized the church in Parsonsfield in 1785 and continued to preach and cultivate his farm in that town until January, 1793, when on returning to his home from a meeting in Porter he lost his way in the woods and was so severely frozen that he never afterward regained his full health. During the earlier years of his life Elder Weeks was a mechanic, but always of pious mind, he fitted himself for the ministry, and was ordained pastor of the Baptist church at Gilmanton, June 15, 1780. He accepted the teachings of the Free Will Baptist church after his removal to Parsonsfield. He stood six feet four inches in height, was broad shouldered and possessed a very strong voice: and indeed he was a powerful man in every sense and was not wanting in physical courage, as may be inferred from the following anecdote which is related of him: "On his way to meet an appointment in Limerick he came to a bridge upon which two men were standing. They told him to 'go home, for he was no minister, and could not pass.' He quietly turned his horse, but soon returned, bearing aloft a stake, calling out: 'The Lord told me to go to Durgin's and preach. If you attempt me I will split your heads.'" He was permitted to pass without further molestation. Elder Weeks married (first) Mercy Randlett, and by her had twelve children. Married (second) Mrs. Sarah Barnes, whose family name was Guptail. She bore him one child.

Nathaniel F Weymouth
Birth:
Oct. 3, 1818
Gray, Maine
Death:
Oct. 1, 1887
Burial:
Rogers Cemetery
Troy
Waldo County, Maine

He was licensed in September, 1852 at the age of 34. After this, he was a student five terms at New Hampton, New Hampshire mostly during his 38th year. He was ordained June 18, 1857 by the Exeter Quarterly Meeting. His pastorates were basically in the Exeter area. The Exeter church was organized during his pastorate there. He also assisted in the organization of several churches and had revivals at Exeter, Pittsfield and Burnham. He gave liberally in the building of churches and for the Maine Central Institute of which he was a trustee. He was also clerk of the Exeter Quarterly Meeting for 12 years. He married Judith P. (Simons) in 1843.

Samuel Wheeler
Birth:
May 20, 1801
Chesterville, Maine
Death:
Apr. 6
Burial:
Chesterville Center Cemetery
Chesterville
Franklin County, Maine

His grandfather came to the United States from England about 1770 and served in the Revolutionary War with courage and gallantry under Commodore John Paul Jones. Mr. Wheeler became a Christian at the age of 17 and was licensed in June, 1841. He was Ordained at Vienna, Maine the following year in June by a Council of the Farmington Quarterly Meeting. He pastored numerous churches in the area. However, he was the most successful as a pastor that Chesterville church which he pastored for 40 years. In 1864 he represented his town in the legislature. He married to November 11, 1823 to Miss Nancy W. Keniston.

Simeon Coffin Whitcomb	Joseph White

Simeon Coffin Whitcomb
Birth:
Jan. 16, 1845
Thorndike, Waldo County, Maine
Death:
Feb. 24, 1918
Bangor,Penobscot County, Maine
Burial:
Mount Hope Cemetery
Bangor
Penobscot County, Maine

He was a student at Hampden, Maine where he studied at the Academy and later at Maine State Seminary. In 1862, he enlisted in the Army as a private and rose to a second sergeant before the close of the war. At age 22, he was converted and soon felt called to preach. He was licensed in September 1874. He graduated from Bangor Theological Seminary and was ordained at Dover, Maine on July 1, 1875. He held a number of successful pastorates and became a trustee of the Maine Central Institute, Pittsfield, and was clerk of the Maine Central Yearly Meeting. On August 1, 1877 he was married to Miss Celestia Cates.

Joseph White
Birth:
May 24, 1789
Standish, Maine
Death:
May 17, 1837
Burial:
Harding Cemetery
Standish
Cumberland County, Maine

At the age of 20 he witnessed a baptismal of 150 in his town by the Rev.'s Z. Leach and Silas Hutchison. As Leach was coming up out of the water, he noticed a young man of serious face gazing earnestly and said, "come now and let us reason together saith the Lord." These words God blessed to the conversion of Joseph White. In 1814, he became deeply impressed with Colby's petition for help in Rhode Island, and in company with Rev. George Lamb on May 1, 1815 he set out for this field, which for the next 10 years was to be so richly blessed by his ministry. He joined John Colby and for three months they preached together there and in surrounding towns. He returned to Maine and was ordained on November 4 at a session of the yearly meeting held in Fort Hill in Gorham. During the next 22 years of his ministry he was engaged in the Master's work. By June, he left the state to visit the yearly meeting in New Hampshire and make a tour in Maine, at his home administering his first baptism. A little previous to Colby's death in 1817, Colby urgently solicited White to re-visit Rhode Island. A revival attended his efforts at Parsonsfield, Maine. For the next six years he spent most of his time in Rhode Island. On May 16, 1820 he organized the First Smithfield church at Greenville which prospered greatly under his care. At the Rhode Island meeting in October, 1821 the church numbered 144 members. He presented the organization of the quarterly meeting and at that time assisted in the ordination of the first Free Baptist minister ordained in the state. He was greatly used in his state and neighboring states. He was a member of the sixth and seventh General Conferences. With John Buzzell, Henry Hobbs, Enoch Place and Hosea Quinby. He was chosen by the General Conference on the committee of revision for the denominational treatise published in 1834. Two days before his death he said, "I find support in the Christian religion, my soul rest in the bosom of God." And also, "life is none too good to wear out in the service of God." He first married Elizabeth White (1796 - 1863) day next year after their marriage leave you a baby child. Thereafter he married her sister, Catherine White (1798 - 1822).

Thomas White, II
Birth:
1806
York County
New Brunswick, Canada
Death:
Dec. 19, 1859
Hodgdon, Maine
Burial:
Hodgdon Cemetery
Hodgdon
Aroostook

He was converted in 1822 uniting with the Christian church in his location. In 1829 he married and moved a Hodgdon where he joined the Free Baptist church under the evangelistic labors of Elder's Leonard Hathaway and Stillson. In 1840, he was called to God and entered the Christian ministry. He was ordained in 1853. Note: Marker placed beside stone by GAR.

Rev John Ansel Wiggin

Birth:
Jul. 2, 1859
Baldwin
Cumberland County
Maine, USA
Death:
Jul. 20, 1930
Burial:
Eastern Cemetery
Gorham
Cumberland County
Maine, USA

Rev. John Ansel Wiggin, son of John and Martha A. (McKenney) WIGGIN, was born at North Baldwin, Maine. In January 1875, he was converted. He graduated from Nichols Latin School in 1882, and from Cobb Divinity School in June 1887. In July 1884, he was licensed, and was ordained July 21, 1887, by the Anson Quarterly Meeting as pastor of the church in Madison. At the same time Rev. R.B. Hutchins, at the request of the Lexington church was ordained, the Rev. A.T. Salley preaching the sermon.

Because He Lives
All Fear Is Gone

Stephen Williamson

Birth:
Feb. 16, 1795
Maine
Death:
Jul. 2, 1873
Stark
Somerset County, Maine
Burial:
Tupper-Williamson Cemetery
Starks, Somerset County, Maine

Williamson, died in Stark, Me., his native town. When twenty-one years of age he became a Christian and united with the First church in Stark. He was licensed to preach Aug. 10, 1822 and again by the Farmington Q. M. Feb. 5, 1824. Dec. 4, 1826, he was ordained. He labored successfully in many revivals, particularly at New Portland, Anson, Mercer and Stark. In business he was wise and successful and the benevolent causes found in him sympathy and support. He was a friend of freedom and temperance. His name is frequently found on the records of Q. M's, Y. M's and General Conferences.

Ezra Winslow
Birth:
Apr. 13, 1808
New Vineyard, Franklin County,
Maine
Death:
Jul. 27, 1884
New Portland, Somerset County,
Maine
Burial:
West New Portland Cemetery
New Portland,
Somerset County, Maine

He was the son of Rev. Howard, an M.E. minister, and Polly Winslow. He was an acceptable teacher for many years. His conversion in early life was thorough. He joined the M.E. class and was soon licensed by "camp-meeting" John Allen. Having become convinced that baptism should be by immersion only, he took a letter and joined the Free Baptists.He was united in marriage with Miss Mary Thomas, of Farmington, March 24, 1831.He was ordained by a council appointed by the Anson Quarterly Meeting in June 1850. His labors were in many towns in Somerset and Franklin counties, and were abundant and fruitful.He

remembered each of the benevolent causes of the denomination in his will. He died at age 76 years, 3 months.

Lewis H Witham
Birth:
July 6, 1817
Milton, N. H.
Death:
Jan. 26, 1880
Biddeford, Me.
Burial:
Woodlawn Cemetery
Biddeford, York County, Maine

His father was Obadiah Witham, of Wakefield, N. H., and his mother, Abigail Hanson, of Milton. He was a teacher in a large number of schools. In 1834 he became a Christian, and three years later began to preach. He was licensed the next year, and was ordained Sept. 13, 1839, by the Waterboro Q. M. Rev. H. Hobbs preached the sermon. In 1840 he was married to Miss Martha A. Richardson, of Limington. He spent some time in missionary work in his Q. M., and supported himself by teaching. During his ministry he baptized 182 persons: fifty in Saco, forty-one in Biddeford, twenty-six in South Buxton, and the others in Kennebunk, Kennebunk Port, Hollis, Lyman, and Lebanon, Me., Portsmouth, and Contoocookville, N. H., and two in Bristol, Pa., while connected with the army. He enlisted in the Thirty-second Maine Volunteers in February, 1864, and finally acted as chaplain.

Through ill health he was mustered out of service in

July, 1865. He was pastor at Shapleigh two years, and South Buxton six years. He preached six months at Kittery, and was supplying at Kennebunk Port when he was prostrated by the disease which resulted in his death. He was clerk of the Maine Western Y. M. twelve years.

John Whitney
Birth:
Unknown
Death:
Mar. 9, 1851
Burial:
Elmwood Cemetery
Dexter
Penobscot County, Maine

In June 1785, to attend the Q. M., and there related his Christian experience and call to the ministry. The question of his ordination was referred to the next Q. M., when it was decided in the affirmative, and he was ordained at Westport, Sept. 7; Randall himself preached the sermon, Tingley made the consecrating prayer, and Hibbard gave the hand of fellowship. He was the first to be ordained to the ministry in the denomination, and for thirty years he was successful especially in awakening sinners in his evangelistic work. He frequently met with opposition in his preaching tours. He visited the frontier settlements with Tingley the year of his ordination, and souls were saved and a few churches organized. He went to reside at Edgecomb, where a church of twenty members was organized by the aid of Hibbard. In 1787 a remarkable revival was enjoyed by him at Royalsborough. In 1788 he baptized several at Lewiston and visited the "Eastern country." He moved his family to Leeds, where they resided for several years. He organized churches at Canaan, Bristol, aild at the present Camden. In 1791 from the revival in Kittery, a church, vas embodied. In September, 1793, with Randall, Tingley, Hibbard, and Deacon Otis he went from the Y. M. to answer the call for help from the churches in the Sandy River valley. In 1813 he moved to Newfield, and through faithful labors the place of death soon bloomed as a garden. One hundred and fifty were converted during the year. Samuel Burbank, the teacher, with many pupils was among the number.

William Woodsum
Birth:
Feb. 1, 1792
Saco
York County, Maine
Death:
Jul. 24, 1872
Dickvale
Oxford County, Maine
Burial:Dickvale Cemetery
Dickvale
Oxford County, Maine

He was converted at the age of sixteen and soon felt called to preach, but being an orphan and having little education he put it off until he should be settled in life.In January, 1814, he married Miss Rosannah Woodman, of Leeds, Me. They had eleven children.He soon began with trembling to preach the gospel. He was ordained in Sumner, Sept. 20, 1823 (and there for about 17 years). Many were led to Christ through his efforts. In 1831 he settled in Peru, and resided there till his death. History shows that he founded the Free Baptist Church there, and he was its pastor for nearly 40 years. He also preached in various places in Maine and New

Hampshire, attending about four hundred funerals. He repeatedly served his town in public offices, and in 1833, he represented his district in the Legislature.

Samuel Wormwood
Birth:
Jun. 24, 1793
Saco, York County, Maine
Death:
Mar. 25, 1865
North Berwick
York County, Maine
Burial:
Mount Pleasant Cemetery
North Berwick, York County,
Maine

He was converted and baptized by Rev.John Buzzell when about eighteen years old, and at the age of twenty-one was ordained. Meeting with opposition in his early Christian life, he yet stood firm and -remained true. His labors were confined mostly to the Wellington Q M. on the St. John River. In Brighton seventy were converted under his labors in about three weeks. At that time another baptized the candidates, as Brother Wormwood was afflicted with lameness from which he never afterwards was free. His life was characterized by the spirit of true piety, sound doctrine, and indomitable perseverance. He moved his family to North Berwick two years before his death, where his health gradually declined.

Psalm 90:5-6, "You sweep men away in the sleep of death; they are like the new grass of the morning-though in the morning it springs up new, by evening it is dry and withered."